Copyright © 2023 Val Griffiths
All rights reserved
No part of this book may be reproduced, or stored in a retrieval system,
or transmitted in any form or by any means, mechanical, electronic,
or otherwise, without the express written permission of the author.
Cover design by Val Griffiths

This book is dedicated to my son, Dan.
The greatest teacher of unconditional love ....
Love brought us together
Love holds us together
Ours is a love story that never ends....

Prologue

It wasn't easy writing the prologue for this book and it's fair to say, I made several attempts at it.
In all honesty, I didn't even expect to be writing this book,
but one day, back in the spring of 2021 I heard my son announce...
'Mum...you're going to write a book!'
My son had been spirit side since April 30th 2019
and by now, I was well accustomed to hearing him telepathically.

As I recall the memory of that day, it was the second anniversary of his passing
and I was with my two older children, Dan's siblings, walking along the seafront near home.
I turned to them and announced... 'I've got to write a book, Dan's just told me.'
And at that moment, the idea for this book was born.
This is not a book about me and my son, though you will learn a little bit about us through these words.
It's a book about my journey with grief. How I've navigated the many storms we all face,
and learned so much about life and 'death' along the way.
It is my hope that these words will touch the hearts of others
who have suffered the loss of a loved one.
Whether you are just setting out on this path, or have been on it for a long time,
I hope the words contained herein, bring about some peace.

But first, a little introduction to my son and the reason this book came to life.
He was 'given' the name Daniel when he was born, but we all called him Danny as a youngster.
Later in life, he shortened his name to Dan, announcing that he preferred it.
When I say he was '<u>given</u>' the name Daniel, I wonder if you'd believe me if I told you
that he actually <u>chose</u> his own name long before he arrived on this earth plane?
Not possible some may say? But actually, he did!
There may be things I write about in these pages, that will perhaps stir some memories in you the reader.
You may read things you've never considered before,
or things you simply don't believe in....
Grief has called me to suspend my beliefs on more than one subject and on more than one occasion
and I have learnt to go along with it, just to see where it would take me.
I've certainly become much more open minded about life and death and everything
in-between....and beyond, since my son's passing.
So I invite you to keep an open mind if you can, as you read through these pages.

But I digress....I already had two children before Dan made his appearance.
A girl and a boy and I didn't plan on having any more children. As far as I was concerned,
my family was complete. I would find out years later, that what I thought of as 'my plans',
were never mine to begin with, but that I, as are we all,
was part of a much bigger picture.

cont....

...cont

One evening I was watching a movie. I can't remember the name of it,
but I do remember that it had a little boy in it called Daniel
and I was suddenly overcome with the feeling that when I have another child, he will be called Daniel.
Oh, I thought, that's a nice name, but I don't plan on having any more children,
so I'm not sure where that thought came from and quickly dismissed it.
But it was stored in my memory bank.
Fast forward a few years and I was indeed expecting another child.
I knew instinctively it would be a boy. I didn't need a scan to tell me that...I just knew.
Just as I also knew he would be named Daniel.
After all, he had already told me, years earlier.

When my son was born, in December of 1992,
I was overcome with the feeling that I'd known him before.
That I somehow knew him on a deep soul level.
When the visitors left the hospital ward, I remember picking him up,
cradling him in my arms and saying to him...
'What have you come here for?... Something tells me you have come for a very special reason...'
This strong impression, or 'knowing', hadn't happened with my two older children
and time would indeed tell, just why I felt this way....
and what Daniel/Danny/Dan, had come here for.

I've often found I can express myself best, through the 'written word.'
I filled many journals in the weeks and months following Dan's death.
When I look back on them now, I can see the sheer range of emotions that grief was taking me on.
Writing in my journals helped me to get through some really tough days.
At times, it seemed as if the words weren't expressions of mine alone.
I felt there was another presence there with me .... guiding my hand.
I wondered at the time, whether my son was communicating with me,
through this medium of writing, because it was something I felt comfortable with.

I began to acknowledge and thank him for being alongside me
and he began encouraging me to write about and explore things that I hadn't previously explored.
I began asking questions of him and the answers would arise in my mind
and my hand would transfer them onto the page.
Sometimes, I would be surprised when I read back what was written,
as the words certainly felt like they weren't consciously written by me.

So began a new chapter of my journey through life.
A journey with my son in spirit.

cont...

...cont.

As I say, this is a book about my journey with grief thus far ...
And how I've not only managed to survive, but have begun to find meaning in life again, too.
I understand we don't all come from the same backgrounds and as such,
we don't all hold the same beliefs as one another. And in all honesty, my beliefs have,
and continue to evolve, as I experience life and all its hidden mysteries.

I've never followed any particular religion,
but I have always acknowledged that there is a force larger than myself, call it God, Source,
The Universe, Great Spirit....these words I find are easily interchangeable for me.
I also acknowledge that there is more to life than what we experience through our five human senses.
I'm far from knowing everything there is to know and I love that there is so much more to explore,
with my son as my wing-man, my guide and my delightful companion.

There are however, a few things that I've learnt along this journey with grief that I no longer question....
1) Life doesn't end at death,
2) My son is on this journey with me, and
3) Grief is not linear!

Likewise, when it came to organising this book,
I tried to get it into some kind of order ... into some semblance of flow.
But it wasn't working.
Just like grief, it wouldn't fall into a neat timeline...beginning, middle and end.
So I took the advice that grief has been giving me all along
and stopped trying to force it to fit into my idea of what it should be like.
I realise that some days I am writing from a place of deep love and joy and other days,
I am writing from a place of deep grief and despair.
Both are valid and as both are experienced, both needed (or demanded) a voice.

So consequently, you don't have to read this book in page order, from beginning to end,
(though of course you can if you wish).
But rather, it can be opened at any page and the words read and resonated with, ... (or not),
depending on you, the reader and how you are feeling at the time.
I feel it works well this way.

Writing this book has been a deeply cathartic experience for me.
I have visited places in my mind, my heart and my soul,
that I may not have otherwise visited.
I hope some of the words here, bring a little comfort, peace or whatever you, the reader, may need,
as you continue on this difficult journey with grief.

MUCH LOVE AND MANY BEAUTIFUL BLESSINGS TO YOU,
MY FELLOW TRAVELLER,...

Memories

Memories of your tiny fingers holding onto mine, with great strength for one so small.
Memories of funny faces you pulled, to make us laugh ... which always made you laugh too.
Memories of sunny days in the garden with a paddling pool you guarded with your life,
from other children who'd come to play, like you were testing your 3 year old authority...
to see how it would hold up.
Memories of wading in streams and rivers with oversized wellies, and a face filled with wonder
at what lay hidden under the rocks, as your small hands wrestled to find out.
Memories of the village library where you'd choose your books with so much care and attention,
knowing instinctively which ones would light up your inner world.
Memories of nose bleeds, grazed knees, splinters and sore elbows,
from falling off bikes that were far too big.
Memories of cuddles on the sofa and smelling the softness of your hair
....you had such beautiful hair I remember.
Memories of walking the forest path to school each day,
where you'd bend to pick up large black beetles on the path which you feared may get trodden on,
and place them gently into the long grass, out of harms way.
Memories of the tender way you approached animals,
as if you could sense what was going on inside them,
and how they would warm to you in an instant, even on a first meeting.
Memories of deep conversations about life, far more suited to an elder,
with deep knowledge and wisdom.... than a child of 8 or 9.
Memories of questions asked, that I couldn't always answer, like ...
'Why do I float out of my body sometimes, when I'm playing with my friends?'
or
'When I go somewhere I've never been before, why does it feel so familiar'...?
Memories of hospital visits to mend a broken arm, a broken nose and a face so badly burned,
it was a miracle that it left you with no scars to remind you of your recklessness.
Memories of you pulling away from me... of the child in you disappearing into adulthood
and your carefree and determined spirit wanting to explore beyond the boundaries
that could no longer contain you.
Memories of phone-calls...or lack of phone-calls, that alerted me to 'something's wrong'.
Memories of years of worry and fear that life would take you from me,
and you... feeling that you were 'invincible', would be proved wrong in the end.
Memories of THE phone-call.
Memories of what followed.

Memories...... So many memories.
Which ones do I hold onto?
Some beautiful to revisit, some more difficult....
but they all make up the life that we shared.
So I'm learning to embrace them all.

What happens when you lose someone you love?
What happens when their physical presence
is no longer evident in your life?
How does life continue?
How do you go on without them?

What is this thing called grief which comes knocking
on the windows and doors of your life,
with its almighty great fist?

You don't want to answer.
You don't want to let it in.
Yet it pounds and pounds continuously,
to the beat of your fractured heart.

You try to hide behind the sofa
of your previously safe existence.
You hide in the shadows of your desperation
and hope grief doesn't find you there.

But grief doesn't give up that easily.
She sneaks in through the door of your consciousness.
She winds her way around your broken heart
and she squeezes with all of her might
until you feel your heart may burst open
and you will disappear into the void.

You feel you have no choice, but to surrender.
And when you give yourself over completely,
you feel you may just dissolve into the blackness of her presence.
But just before you do, you realise she has loosened her grip.
You can breathe again.
She's not the enemy you thought she was

She may just have come to save you...

How do I begin to tell our story…?
if indeed it needs to be told.

How do I begin to put into words a love so deep
it touches the depth of the ocean floor
and reaches up to dance with the millions of stars
that extend to embrace it
and welcome it as a striking addition to the
beauty of the night sky?

How do I begin to say all that I feel within my heart?
All the joys, all the sorrow, all the laughter amid the challenges,
all the nights of dark despair
that clung to my nightclothes seeking to
drown me in the sweat of my own fears?

How do I begin to describe my desperate pleas to God,
to the Universe, to anyone who would listen,
to rescue me from this mission that I had mistakenly taken on
and give me to something easier….more manageable,
lest I lose myself completely to the blackness
that I could feel, seeping into the crevices
of my very soul,
with its suffocating dreadlocks of doom?

How do I begin to express
the search for meaning among the madness,
in a world that offers only conflicting arguments,
judgements and no concrete and meaningful
'road map' of guidance,
to one who is earnestly searching for truth?

How do I do this alone,
when I feel God and his band of angels have spitefully deserted me
and risen an unreachable octave higher,
lest they get sullied by the discordant sounds
of my sorrow and pain?

How do I reach down into the depth of knowing,
that I feel has been denied to me,
hidden away like the precious pearl of the traitorous oyster
who won't be persuaded to part with it,
even though she knows it may eventually kill her?

How do I begin to tell our story…?

I knew from the very beginning that I had to find out
where my son had gone.
Some may say that I couldn't accept that he'd died,
but it wasn't that at all.
I knew he no longer 'walked the earth' in the way that he once did,
but I also knew, at a deep level,
that he couldn't simply disappear.
I had a belief in the afterlife from a young age.
I suppose one may say it was inherent within me,
its just that most people around me, didn't talk about it.
So when my son passed, I read, listened to
and engaged in anything that I was drawn to ...
... anything that 'felt right' to me.
Anything that could help me understand 'death' on a deeper level.

Coming to the understanding I have today,
has been a process and it certainly didn't happen overnight.
But not a day went by, when I didn't engage in
something to do with the afterlife.
Looking back, I know now, that I was being 'divinely led'.
I know deep within my heart, that there is something much greater than us all,
something that protects, us and leads us on our true path, if we allow it to.
It is a 'something' that is called by many names, yet cannot be fully defined.
And I was simply ready to surrender to whatever could help me move towards healing.

I began talking to my son immediately, asking him to help me understand
where he was, and how I could communicate with him on a regular basis ...
... because I certainly needed to feel in close contact with him.
The more I researched, understood and integrated certain teachings
into my belief system, the better I felt.
The process was definitely helping, so I continued.
And I still continue to learn and grow today.
There were certain things that I read that didn't resonate with me, so I left those aside.
I wasn't going to argue with anyone else's belief systems.
What I was trying to do, looking back, was remember what my Soul already knew.

We simply don't die....
We transform.

ONE DAY

In the beginning....I prayed to God, the Universe, my son...
whoever was listening, to help me get through one day!
Just ONE DAY!

Because if I could survive ONE DAY
with the knowledge of my son's departure from
this world
(I couldn't say death, or dead, or any of those other words
that seemed so final),
then maybe there was a chance that I could survive the next and the next,
and hopefully the next.

I prayed so hard for strength in those early days
and thankfully my desperate pleas were heard.
For I felt a strength I had never felt before,
embody me.

Like a suit of armour it grew around me,
whilst my insides remained soft and vulnerable...

That suit of armour...that protection...
...that strength,
wherever it came from,
kept me safe,
kept me from falling apart.
It was gifted to me when I needed it most.

I still wear it today...

Walking through the dark corridors of grief,
I stumble and fall.
Yet something helps me to rise ...
to get to my feet once again,
when it seems so much easier to remain
in a crumpled heap,
on the floor of my sorrowful and painful existence.
Something helps me up,
and sets me on my unsteady feet,
and I stumble forwards once more,
with soft and gentle words of encouragement
being whispered in my ear....

KEEP GOING ...

Your struggle is real.
But so too, is your strength.

A PAUSE

A pause
to digest information
I never wanted to hear.
If I stayed in this moment
without responding,
could I erase what I was being told?
Could I erase a future,
I knew was right at this moment
opening up?
A future I didn't want to face....
A future I wanted to run from?
Could this pause magically turn back time
to before I answered the phone?

A pause
to digest what was being said.
The words tasted so bitter in my mouth
my body threatened to forcefully eject them.
Time stood still.....
Between now and forever an ocean stood,
threatening to drown me
should I dare move
or breathe
and break the silence.

A pause
Was I drowning already?
Was a chasm even now opening up
into which I could fall and disappear
without trace.
A pause I prayed would last an eternity,
so I'd never have to face
what was to come.

Breaking the news and feeling your presence

My daughter had to break the news to me.
I feel bad for her, that she had to make that phone call to her mother.
She wanted to travel the 180 miles to fetch me as I was working away,
but I insisted I could drive half way to meet her.
Truth was, I had to get moving.
I couldn't stay still with the echoes of her words ringing in my ears...
'My son was dead'.
But the journey wasn't a straight forward one.
It should have been, don't you think?
How can a journey NOT be straight forward at a time like this?
It was nighttime, on an almost deserted motorway.
An incident up ahead and a policeman standing in the road
directing the traffic to turn off at the next exit.
I almost lost my mind at that point, my nerves were so on edge, and my body was shaking.
But I felt my son's presence in the passenger seat next to me.
I had felt him sit on the bed beside me, when my daughter delivered the news.
I can't explain it....I just felt him sitting beside me telling me everything was going to be alright.
I begged him to please give me the strength to get home safely, to the comfort of my family.
So he was doing as I'd asked.
He was sitting beside me as I drove slowly along the darkened highway, willing the journey to end.
I had the radio on. An audio book was playing.
I wasn't listening, but I couldn't bear the silence either.
My thoughts were racing and I struggled to concentrate on the road ahead.
Suddenly, the radio went all crackly like it was being tuned to another station.
My mind snapped back from its wanderings and I asked ....'Was that you?'

In the weeks, months and years ahead, I would ask that same question countless times.
The radio crackled again then returned to the audio book that was playing.
I knew without a doubt, that it was my son and I thanked him for saving my sanity.
In time, I would scold him for messing with anything electronic.
I would tell him..."find another way of communicating, that doesn't involve
messing with my phone, my laptop...the TV etc."
And he would oblige....and switch to messing with his brother and sister's electrics instead!

I drove slowly along, wondering what could be causing the traffic to be moving so slowly
when I was so desperate to get to safety!
Eventually I was able to exit the motorway
and drive until I found a service station a few miles away.
Somewhere my daughter could find me.

cont....

cont.......

As I sat in the coffee shop, with a black coffee warming my hands,
a song came through the speaker system,
and I knew it was another message from my son.

Tears filled my eyes as I heard my son whisper,
'I'm sorry", and not to blame him.
'I could never blame you', I said quietly......as silent tears rolled down my cheeks.
At that time, I didn't know what had taken my son from this world into the next.
I only knew of how he had struggled with mental health and addiction, for many years,
and how had been using various substances to 'help him feel normal'.

Mental health is so fragile .....so very, very fragile.
I only knew, as I sat there awaiting my daughter's arrival,
that my son had told me a few days previously,
that he didn't think he could go on living anymore,
that life was just too hard.
His girlfriend had just ended their relationship, and this had crushed him.
He told me he didn't love himself .... and his words broke my heart.
These were some of the last words he spoke to me.

I'd asked him to try to hang on if he could.
I told him I loved him enough for both of us.
I told him how wonderful he was and how life could get better.....
if given a chance.
But a part of me knew he didn't believe that.
A part of me knew that he may not be able to survive this period of his life...
a part of me knew that life for him had often been difficult,
locked in addiction with a desire to break free, yet unable to do so.

.........A part of me expected that phone call.

So as I sat with my coffee warming my hands,
listening to the words of the song,
I whispered...
'I could never blame you...
you fought as hard as you could...
And now your struggles are over' ...

... And I knew, mine were just beginning.

In all honesty, I didn't know how I was going to survive.
I didn't know how I was going to go on living, in a world without you in it.
When I woke up that morning ....
the morning after the day my world fell apart,
I didn't have a clue how I was going to survive.

You took so much of me with you,
that day you took your leave,
and left me with almost nothing to hold on to.

I remember thinking, how was I ever going to do
'normal things' again?
Like going to the shops,
or even getting out of bed every morning.
I didn't know.
I just didn't know.

But when I woke that morning, what I did know,
was that Grace must have whispered to me in my sleep
She must have told me that somehow
I WOULD be able to do all of these things
......eventually....just not all at once....

Some days, I may only have the strength to get out of bed.
Another day I may have the strength to get out of bed and walk to the shops.
And one day...far off in the distant future,
I may get out of bed and go back to work
and go shopping in my lunch break.
But not today...

Today I couldn't think of doing anything at all.
Today, I wanted to turn back the hands of time
and rewrite yesterday with a different ending.
An ending with you still in it.
Today, I wanted to do the impossible.

Tomorrow, I may get out of bed....

I didn't expect to die the day you did.
I didn't expect the breath to leave my body so forcefully.
I didn't expect the life to drain out of me,
like it was being sucked into the parched earth
that I felt no longer supported or sustained me.

I didn't expect to NOT feel anything,
not even pain or sorrow in that moment.
In that moment, it was as if life itself didn't exist.
It was as if I had been disconnected.
The plug had been pulled.... by some unseen hand
and suddenly I was no more.

The blackness of the void...
I'd heard it spoken about...
The nothingness...
The silence....
No coming or going
No past or present.
No me or you.
Nothing but silence.

Then something inside me stirred to the echo of a faint and distant cry.....
did I hear it, or feel it.... ?
rising up from a place I wasn't even aware existed.
I instinctively knew if it reached the surface,
it had the power to shatter the toughest of glass...
to shatter the very fabric of my life as I knew it
and tear it to shreds.
So I stopped it somehow.
I silently erected a damn to hold back the tidal wave of tears that I knew was to come.
I held things together,
lest I shock and shatter those around me.
I held it in, that silent mournful, hollow cry....
and swam up from the clutches of the void with a pain buried so deep within me,
I would need grief to show me how to reach it.

And she did and she continues to do so...

My son.....

He wasn't perfect by any means...
But then who is?
He wasn't bothered about education
and thought school was a bit of a bore.
He loved to walk in the woods and wade in streams
and catch butterflies when he was young...
and then let them go.
He liked being out in nature
and the forest seemed to embrace him
He loved visiting old castles to explore ...
like he'd been there before....
in another lifetime perhaps?

He had out of body experiences from 7 years of age....
and premonitions that he spoke to me about.
Wise words often came from his lips.
They seemed out of place in one so young.
He said he never intended to grow old
and like Peter Pan,
he didn't want to grow up.

He was funny and loved to make people smile
He had a mischievous grin and his laugh....
you could always recognise him by his laugh.
He didn't take life too seriously.
'Life is for living' he would tell me
He was always rushing onto the next thing
that attracted his attention
like he knew he had a limited amount of time
to fit everything in.

He broke his nose, his arm and badly burned his face
all in the same year...by not 'being careful'.
He lived on the edge,
squeezing as much out of life as he could.
And when he had done that...he left.

cont...

cont...

He loved dogs and cats and all animals.
He could talk to them
more than he could his own kind sometimes.

He also loved LOUD music!
And pizza, burgers,
cheese and mayonnaise...
And banofee pie!

When he was young, he loved Ninja hero turtles....
And The Little Mermaid movie,
which we watched together,
too many times to remember ...
though he may not thank me for sharing that!

He was never pushy,
yet he had a way of getting what he wanted
without you even noticing.
He was hard to say no to....
He had a way about him that could charm the birds from the trees.
"Any chance?" was his catch phrase.

He was an easy child to raise
never wanting for much,
mostly content with what he was given.
He disliked unfairness
Kindness was what he liked...and showed.
His friends called him a legend.
He will live on in many hearts...
Especially mine.
I am fortunate to feel his presence.
Death is but a new chapter
in the book of the life we share.

We catch up with each other
in the crosswinds and we walk forward together,
in our never-ending story
shining light wherever we go....

Every night, I light a candle for you....
I find comfort in this simple ritual.....

In the silence

In the beginning, there was silence.
A silence so deep, I wondered whether the whole world
had ceased to exist without me being aware.
What shadow had I been hiding in, that I hadn't seen it coming?
The shadow of ignorance I learned, is a place we all find comfort in.
Some of us remain there forever, never venturing outside of the door of our created reality
...a reality built on false promises of security and safety,
a false sense of greatness in something that won't do our bidding, no matter how much is promised.
But for me, the door was now open, and Grief was beckoning me
to come out from the shadow of my former self,
......an invitation to step into my true greatness.
I hesitate.
The door remains open...but for how long?
If I don't step through , how long will it wait?
Whatever is behind this door, will it wait forever for my hesitation to dissolve and for me to make a choice?
A choice to stay and run with the direction of the crowd,
without a clue where I am running to...or why,
or to step off the path that I created with other people's ideas of how my life should be,
and rely only on my inner compass for guidance.
Was it now or never?
Would it close?....that door that seemed to have no hidden agenda, no enticing musicality,
only a silence so deep it may just swallow me up in my entirety
and render everything I had ever known
as useless fodder for a world that was built on greed and striving
and complete ignorance to the truth of who we truly are.
Would it close without me ever having known the possibilities and opportunities that lay beyond?
Why was I hesitating?
What was I waiting for?
What was this feeling deep within me that was urging me to step forward boldly,
while another was keeping me rooted to the spot.
Why was I so afraid?
Fear I realised in that moment, had been my constant companion throughout life.
It had taken up residence in the home of my existence and it was not going to be evicted
without a fight.
Fear, I realised in that instance, had stopped me doing so many things I could have done with my life.
Fear had kept me small...not allowing me to grow into the true fullness and fragrance of myself.
Not allowing me to grow into the 'person' I intended to be.
Now fear was keeping me rooted to the spot again.
It sent its dark and creeping tendrils down from the grip it had held on my heart ,
and out through the soles of my feet,
where they dug deep into the earth and tried to render me immobile.
But the door beckoned once more and the grip of fear had momentarily let go of my heart
and the image of what lay behind the door came into view.
And I knew
I simply had to walk through.

My son reassures me....

'Death is only a temporary separation',
'In fact', he says,
'it's no separation at all.
Some talk about me being in 'the other room,'
in truth', he says...
'there is no dividing wall.'

The thing I discovered early on about grief,
is that it is often invisible to others.
It's hidden deep within us
And I sometimes wonder
how and why we hide our grief so well,
instead of sharing it.

I feel there may be a number of reasons.

The most common one perhaps,
is that we don't want to upset those around us,
those that we care about.
Or maybe we feel
we should be doing 'better'
than we believe we are,
Or we get the impression that the people around us
think that we should be doing better,
and that puts pressure on us,
.....so we hold back on sharing how we feel.
Or maybe our experiences have led us to believe
that people generally don't understand
how we feel,
so we decide to keep quiet,
hiding a part of us
that needs to be expressed.
We may believe,
that by putting on a brave face,
we can somehow cheat grief
into taking a back seat,
(which she may indeed do...for a while).

But grief is continually letting me know
that it is healthy to express how I feel
and she tells me it can be done
in a way that need not bring into question,
any of the above.

I ask her to show me......

Dear Grief...
"I'm trying so darned hard today,
but in truth,
I just want to stop the world
and get off!
I know that's not possible....
but....."
'What about a walk in the fresh air'? Grief replies.
'Or a bar of chocolate'?
I settle for a bar of chocolate and a warm blanket
to wrap around me.
Facing my feelings can wait for another day.

There are so many questions that arise within us,
in the early weeks and months after someone dear to us dies.

Questions like ...why did this happen?
.... How will I ever manage?
.... What do I do now?
... How do I navigate these feelings I have ?
... How will I cope ?
... What does the future hold ?
All these questions are perfectly normal
and have been asked by people like us, countless times before.

Answers may come in time ...
... or they may not come at all.
But somehow, in our own time,
we begin to find our way through the mine-field
that has opened up in front of us.

Being gentle on oneself is essential.
Things take a while to sink in.
Yet if I look back now, I can see that
each step of the way , 'the way' appeared.
Things that needed to be organised, got organised.
People showed up when I needed them.
Some stayed ... Some left in a hurry.
Slowly but surely life settled down
and gave me the space to breathe,
and the space to grieve.

Those impossible early days, thankfully don't last forever....
And one day you may find yourself asking a different question, like ...

'Is that you?'
as you feel the presence of your loved one beside you.

I find grief cannot easily be defined in words....
It has to be experienced.
And even then,
if I try to describe my feelings to someone,
they differ from one day to the next,
or even one hour to the next!
"So how do I understand what I'm dealing with"? I cry out in desperation.
Grief answers....
'Be patient'
'Trust'
'Don't try so hard'.

When I experienced this deep dark blackness of grief,
I really did think it might just destroy me.
The intensity was so unlike anything I had ever experienced before,
and I felt I had no place to go...no place to out-run it...no place to hide,
because it was coming from deep within me.
It was spreading throughout my whole body, like a volcano,
threatening to erupt.

The car became my 'safe place', to let these deep emotions out.
I knew I couldn't possibly hold them in forever.....
I knew that for certain.
And I couldn't 'erupt' in front of anyone either.
I knew this would frighten them.
So my car became my place of safety...my sanctuary.

Here, in the solitude of my car, I would drive somewhere remote,
park up and let the emotions inside of me erupt.
I'd picture those women I'd seen long ago,
on the news on my TV-screen,
all dressed in black,
wailing, wailing....wailing over the death of someone they loved.
......And now I knew their pain.

This was no ordinary pain.
This was something much more primitive and it produced a unique sound all of its own.
I called it <u>The primal scream</u>....

It began in the unexplored depths of my being
and found its way up through my body and out of my vocal cords.
I sat there and wailed.
I don't know for how long,
but when it was over, I felt a shift.

I was exhausted.
I was weary.
But I felt relief.....

Grief has since told me, that this is a very healing thing to do..

*Some days are blank.....a blur...
I'm in a cocoon...protected perhaps?*

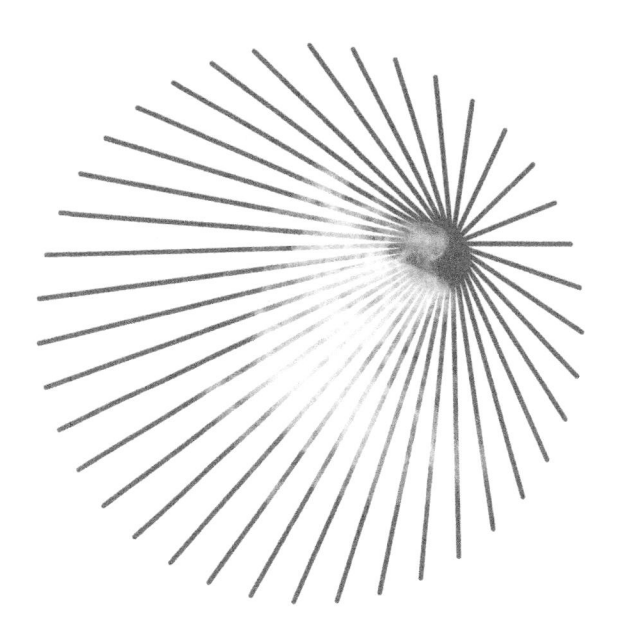

Grief assures me that all of this is natural.....

Life goes on....

Life still goes on even when we would have it stop....
to allow us in the very least, to catch our breath...
There are so many practical things we have to address
in the middle of our shock and disbelief.
What about work? I hear myself absently say to anyone who may be listening.
Living alone, I was my only means of support.

When I do some research, I find, there is no automatic 'paid' bereavement leave
in the UK. It is at the your employer's discretion.
A few years later, the law is changed to grant two weeks bereavement leave,
to parents of children under 18, or pregnancies past 24 weeks.
This age range wouldn't have helped me as sadly they excluded my son..and my grief.
I wondered at the logic behind this....
As if someone had deduced that it was less traumatic, to lose an adult child....

My employer, though sympathetic, grants me 7 days compassionate leave.
I take in a deep breath, as my hand grips the phone.
I am doing a lot of that lately, I've noticed....
sudden sharp intakes of breath...
As if my lungs are trying to make up for the lack of oxygen
I had unknowingly been denying them ...
7 days?
Had I heard correctly?
"Your funeral isn't for another 3 weeks!" I whisper to you.

I have no option but to take unpaid leave for the foreseeable future.
How could I even think of returning to work with you gone from this world?
It seemed inconceivable to ever consider normal life again.
I could hardly function, let alone work.
Fortunately, I had savings to support me,
but I understand not everyone does.

It was a sharp reminder to me of how, as a society, we understand little
about the desperate plight of those who are grieving.

This was one of the many things I would discover on my journey with grief,
in a society that lacks understanding.

Each day brings with it the challenge
of choosing the right thoughts,
the right words to soothe
my aching heart.

Self-Love becomes
so crucial
when one is grieving.
It's as if our bodies
are crying out for a release from
the heartache.
Treat yourself with kindness
You need it now,
more than ever.

Acceptance?

For those still in the early weeks and months of loss,
it takes time to accept our new reality.
And that's OK ... Much grief is expressed and released in these early days.

Acceptance feels difficult.
There are many reasons why we may not want to,
or indeed be able to, accept that our loved one has 'gone'.

We may feel that by doing so, they will somehow
move further away from us and we don't want that.

Another belief we may hold is
'if I accept this, it will be like losing them all over again.'
Or ' if I accept this, it will feel like I'm saying
I didn't love them enough".

It's as if our conscious mind is holding fast to
the non-acceptance, as a means to prove
how much, or how deeply we loved.

Once I realised that NOTHING could diminish how much
I loved and still love my son, I began to let go of these false beliefs
and accept the 'reality' I found myself in.
I certainly didn't like it, I hated it, and wanted to run from it....
but on a deep level, I felt it was important I accept it.

Then, I began to examine what I could 'do' with my new reality.
I began to look for and FIND my son, IN this new reality with me.
I felt if I focused on the absence of him,
it was difficult to focus on his 'presence',
and I knew he was present with me and that's where I had to 'meet him.'
I may not have been able to see or feel his physical presence any longer,
but I began to explore his spiritual presence....his new reality
which I came to understand, is our true essence....
Our Spirit.....Our true self.
I accepted that he was now in his spirit form.
And acceptance began to take on a whole new meaning....and in time,
it brought me a degree of peace, that I so desperately needed.

In my continued search for understanding,
I join a few online grief support groups.
They aren't groups where we talk about
how our loved ones died, over and over again.
I couldn't bear that.
I don't want to revisit that day... It's much too painful.
They are groups that share my belief in the afterlife.
They are a lifeline I cling to and find strength and comfort in.
I know I want to heal this broken heart of mine.
I know I want to find out more than I already know,
about how to reach you wherever you are.
I know you are trying too.
I feel your efforts to reach me
through the thick blackness of my grief.
And I thank you for that.
I feel you are leading me to all the right places,
the right books, the right groups,
the right pieces of information that will help me on this journey.
And I collect them all and piece them together
like a jigsaw puzzle.
I don't have a picture on the box to follow,
but I do have you.
And I know that you can see the bigger picture.
And I trust you to lead the way.

When grief threatens to overtake you
Just remember...
It's grip won't last forever.

This is something I learnt from grief in the early days.....
Even if you feel you will never swim up to the surface again,
as the waves keep pushing you down with their intensity and their strength
and you feel like you're in a small boat,
being tossed around in a tempest......remember
This will also change....

This is what grief taught me in the early days.
I turned it into a mantra that I kept repeating to myself over and over again,
until it was written into the fabric of my very being...
with indelible ink.

.......This will also change......

Because the truth is, even though we experience this crushing pain,
this struggle for breath, over and over again, we are still here...
still breathing.

No pain, however intense and unbearable, lasts forever.
Soon, the icy grip that grief has on you, will be loosened,
and you will be able to breathe more easily again.

Until then, just surrender.
Surrender to the pain of your loss.
Surrender to the emotions that have to have expression.
Don't be afraid you'll get lost in those waves.
We are never alone.
We will never be left alone.
We have what I call our 'spirit team' watching over us, comforting us.
If you listen carefully, they are whispering...hold on...everything will be OK.
You are loved
You are safe
You are protected
You are grieving...

Give yourself the grace to grieve
Give yourself the grace to heal....

Grief tells me she doesn't want to destroy me.
'But it feels that way sometimes,' I whisper ...
She explains gently, that she is there to help me express my emotions.
'Emotions build up like a pressure cooker,' she says,
'and they need to be released.'
She tells me she will help me to express these emotions
in a wholesome way.
She explains she isn't here to destroy me,
but to gently lead me along this path towards healing.

So I take her by the hand...
and I've been holding on, ever since.

Your tenderness arrived unexpectedly that day, but as always, it was timely and welcome.
You always seem to know when I need that special lift, that only your presence can create.
I was barely awake, still groggy from a sleep that had come late that night...
It seems to be that way sometimes.
Sleep...I yearn for its refuge, yet it seems to hide like a minnow, darting behind a rock,
when a child's net is cast into the stream, trying to evade capture.
I was watching the sun glint through the blinds,
casting shadows on the collage of photographs of you, that hang on the wall.
Your chubby face at 2 years old, grinning at someone unseen,
who's trying successfully, to make you smile for the camera.
Your serious face at 8 years old, concentrating hard on winning a conker competition in the town square,
against someone twice your age.....and height !
The moody teenage face, posing for a family photograph you didn't want to be in...
but I'm so glad you are.
That big wide grin of yours in a selfie that you took at the edge of a forest path,
not long before you left this world...
I often wondered where you were going that day...You looked so happy.
That photo is a beautiful reminder that you had a smile that could turn up the brightness
to full beam, in any room you entered.

It was a tap on the window pane that caught my attention, and I slowly moved my gaze,
curious to see what was causing the unfamiliar sound.
A female thrush sat perched, on the windowsill...tapping her beak against the glass.
A smile formed on my lips as I took in the beauty of her mottled breast and the delicate way
she cocked her head to one side, listening and waiting...
almost as if she were inviting a reply to her knocking.
Tap, tap, tap....then again, the head cocked curiously to one side...listening intently, for a response.

I knew at once it was you and the room seemed to shimmer and shift.
'Hello darling' I said. 'You seem to have mastered the art, at last'.
I'm sure I heard you chuckle.
Previous attempts to send signs through these delicate flying creatures,
had seen birds hurl themselves at my window, scaring me half to death!
Poor things I'd say.....Try to be more careful next time, though I was always enthralled
at the things you'd do... to get my attention ...to let me know you were there.

And now, you seem to have mastered the art.
And before you released that bird, from your much more delicate control,
you had it tap twice more on the kitchen window, to get me out of bed.
You're just showing off now, I laughed.
But thank you for your visit and the amazing start to my day.

Grief is unpredictable, messy, and sometimes scary.
When great waves come out of nowhere, it's as much as one can do sometimes,
to hold on and pray they will pass quickly,
because the ferocious storms can feel too much to bear.
I wonder in all honesty, how I, or anyone can survive the battering of these
gigantic waves that seem relentless and determined to destroy me.
Yet even through the desperate wailing of my broken heart,
the racked sobs that echo in my chest,
I hear a faint voice, reassuring me I will be OK.
And I cling to it.
Amplifying each word.
The sound is the sweetest thing I've ever heard.
I don't know its origin, but I trust it somehow.
I feel a protectiveness forming a shield around me.
And in that moment...
I am in the eye of the storm and I am able to regain perspective.
I'm able to right myself and my feet find firm ground once again.

I know there will be more waves to come,
but having weathered this particular storm
and feeling the loving support around me,
my faith has been restored....for the moment.

They say death is a transformation
So when you transformed
I had no choice but to transform too.
How could I remain as I was when I could hear you calling so softly
from the air around me,
asking that I not blame you for leaving, that I not become tainted, or bitter by loss.
I wasn't bitter though.
And I didn't blame you.
How could I be bitter when you gave me so much sweetness in life?
How could I blame you when you suffered so much?
How could I question that life was unfair,
when there were loved ones dying every minute,
and someone was out there.... grieving for them?
How could I question the life that you lived?
A life that was still being lived by many with the same struggles as you had,
in a world that didn't understand them...
In a world that they in turn, didn't understand?
Put things into perspective you said.
So I did.
I sat that first night of your departure, in silent meditation
What I was trying to achieve, I don't know.
I only knew I had questions and I was seeking answers...
answers that may take a lifetime to come.
Hadn't I begged God to release you from your suffering so many times?
Hadn't I pleaded to take on your suffering as my own if it would spare you the pain?
So now, here we are...
You and I
You...free from suffering
And me.....?
Did God hear me after all?
Is He waiting in the wings with the Angels,
to see how I bear this suffering that I begged to carry for you?
Is He watching to see if like Atlas ... the Mythical Greek God,
I can shoulder the weight of this world without you?
Is He eager to see if I can pluck some goodness from the bowl of rotten fruit
that seems to have been placed before me?
Is he curious to know if I can find a diamond among the shards of glass
from a fragile heart that has broken into a million pieces?
Is He hoping I will discover a reason among the wreckage....
a purpose in this pain?

Are you there.......watching and waiting too?

A hearse drove by today. I don't like seeing hearses.
They've never caused such a reaction in me before...but today as the hearse drives by,
I'm transported back to the day of your funeral, when a similar hearse, carrying your body,
made its way slowly up the driveway, towards the chapel.
The driveway I remember, was bordered by a magnificent display of spring flowers.
A seasonal explosion of colour and beauty, providing scant contrast, to the pain of loss.
But even though my mind allowed me to acknowledge their beauty,
just a glimpse of the hearse, was enough to make me take flight and
retreat to the sanctuary of the chapel.
I had agreed beforehand that I couldn't possibly walk behind your casket,
as is often the norm in our culture.
I knew it would break me ... and I was trying so hard not to break.
So I left the hundreds of people outside.
Familiar family faces... and many not so familiar, friends of my son's...
dressed in their colourful outfits, blending with the magnificence of the seasonal blooms.
They had a beauty all of their own, which was not lost on me,
and my heart longed to hug each one of them.
But instead, I entered the safety of the chapel and took my seat in the front row.
I kept repeating to myself....'you're not in there, you're not in there, you're not in there',
as I tried desperately to hold myself together.
Then I heard your faint voice in my mind saying, 'No, I'm not in there, I'm out here...look'.
And it was as if an invisible force had taken hold of me and turned my head to the left
as my gaze rested on the beautiful, radiant forest,
visible through the floor to ceiling windows of the chapel,
glinting like a magnificent masterpiece in the sunlight.
A forest you grew up in. A forest we walked every day when you were young.
A forest where you loved to play, finding sticks to use as swords
to cut through the dense foliage in our path.
A forest where we walked our dog each day,
on our way to school.....Oh how you loved that dog.
And I began to smile inwardly at the memories you planted
like precious blooms in my mind.
It had to be inwardly, for how could I possibly smile outwardly on a day like this,
for people to see and not understand what was in my heart...
that I knew without a doubt, that my son was not in that box being carried in,
but free as a bird to soar over the forest that he loved so much.
Wasn't I supposed to be in floods of tears, or at least looking crestfallen?
But at that moment, my son's spirit was with me, lending me his strength,
to get me through this day......just like he promised he would.
So I smiled inwardly to myself.....
and continued to stare out of the window.

The day was bitter sweet.
Many said it was the best funeral they had ever been to
and when their time comes, they want one like yours.

I have to admit it moved me....beyond tears.
There actually weren't many tears that day...
they would come later.
It moved me to see how so very loved you were.
How your friends moved and swayed with the ease of youth.
Even in grief, there was so much joy.
A send off fit for a 'legend' as they called you.

What was it about you that people could relate to?
Young or old, it made no difference...
they all loved you.

I guess some of us are so easy to love and others, not so much.
Maybe you were a vessel of 'love itself'.
It oozed from your pores without any effort at all.
You wore your heart on your sleeve for the whole world to see.
You were a diamond among pieces of broken glass.
Imitation was not available to you.
You simply had to shine....
You entered the darkness to shine your light among those who were suffering.
And you suffered too.
But you bore that suffering with a humility that only you could pull off.
As I say, no imitation was available to you....
you had to be your authentic self
An enigma...
A blessing....
A legend...
An invitation to love, unconditionally in a world
that holds so much hate, fear and betrayal...
You were a light.
Some were able to see it......others not.
But you shone none the less...

We don't need to have it all
figured out
We can trust that we are
always being guided
by our loved ones,
...unseen,
yet ever present...

I knew I wanted to speak at my son's funeral.
I didn't know if I would have the strength at the time,
but I knew I wanted to.
So just one day after my son left this world, these words came flooding into my mind
and I knew immediately that these were the words I needed to say.
I did find the strength that day.
My son made sure of that. He knew how important it was to me.

A Precious Son

From the moment that I saw you,
and held you in my arms,
I knew you were a special Soul
and that we'd never be apart.
Our hearts beat to the same rhythm
the same blood flowed through our veins
You had come here for a reason,
that would never fully be explained.
You touched the lives of many,
that now, is so plain to see,
we never could contain you,
you were determined to fly free.
You had a heart as big as the Ocean,
your love was of the highest kind
and the demons that you battled with
could never fully be defined.
But in this world we all travel,
some things are plain to see
and some are more of a puzzle
and will remain a mystery.
Now that you have journeyed,
much further on your way,
many of us will grieve you,
with an ache that won't fully go away.
But if we want to be near you
for just a little while,
we only have to think of you,
to see your beautiful smile.
For you can never fully leave us...
our hearts are intertwined,
and the legacy that you leave with us is..
If you can be anything ......
"Just be kind".

One day at a time is
often all we can manage...
All the while,
trusting that we will be
given the strength
and shown the way....

It wasn't easy to let you go.
Every fibre of my being said hang on...hang on
but hanging on was futile.
You were already floating, high above the clouds
on your way to a new destination,
a new adventure......a new home.
A song about 'letting go',
I'm told it was a favourite of yours, one I'd never heard .... before,
was playing ...
as I emerged, trance-like,
from the strange protectiveness of the beautiful chapel where I left you.
Its haunting melody opening me up like a sunflower,
to the rays of the spring sunlight....
Lifting me high above the clouds
if only for a moment
so I could catch a glimpse
of where you were going.
Would you look back or would it be too painful ?
Painful for who I thought.
Not you, you were already free....
Already floating....
And then I lifted...
into the air, like a leaf being plucked from the earth by a
sudden up-draft and I was floating too...
out of my body...
out of my troubled mind .... briefly, ever so briefly...
before I drifted back down again,
and became rooted to the earth once more.
'I've lost you', I whispered
"No", you said
"You will never lose me.
I am here.
Let go of how you imagine things to be.
Let go of how you think things ought to be.
Let go of how things used to be.
But don't let go of me...."

The Rose

A Single Rose

grown in life's wondrous garden
Tender petals
Velvet to the touch
Did you care much for flowers?
I imagined not.
Yet with this single flower
I was saying I love you
I cared
With this single flower
I was saying you meant something
Your life mattered
You were loved
With this single flower I was saying
I saw your pain
your struggles
your bravery.
With this single flower I was saying you were seen.
With this single flower with its beauty as well as its thorns
I was saying I recognise life was harsh for you sometimes,
that your path wasn't as smooth as the velvety petals
but littered with sharp edges like the thorns.
With this single flower I was saying
Thank you
Thank you for being in my life.
Thank you for the beautiful moments
that will stay etched in my memory,
providing strength
for the difficult path I knew was ahead.
With this single flower I was saying
your life wasn't in vain.
It wasn't a life wasted, but a life well lived.
With this single flower I was saying
I'm sorry I couldn't give you a reason to stay,
to see if you could catch a break in the clouds
so the sun could shine through and show you
there may be more waiting for you, than you ever knew.
With this single flower I was saying
you were so very, very loved,
by all the broken-hearted people gathered today,
to say a goodbye they never wanted to say.
With this single flower, as I placed it on your casket,
I was saying
....I'm sorry, I couldn't save you.

As a society, we don't seem to know how to relate to grief,
much less those who are grieving.
Perhaps if I wore a black calf length dress
and a black hat and veil,
or a t-shirt emblazoned with the words
GRIEVING!
people would know and maybe understand the pain I am in.

But I look ordinary...the same
Except I'm not the same and I never will be.
Grief is now my constant companion and today...
today she is weighing heavily on my shoulders.

So forgive me if I don't laugh like I used to.
If I don't see the funny side of things anymore.
Forgive me if I seem lost in thought, or absent minded,
like I'm not listening to you when you speak.

Forgive me if I no longer seem interested in things of a trivial nature.
The fact is, most things seem trivial to me now.
Everything pales in comparison when placed beside my son's death.

So please forgive me and bear with me
while I adjust to my new normal...

Grief has a way of changing us.
It pulls us from the comfort of our neatly organised lives,
where we lived when we look back now.... almost carefree,
blissfully unaware of the changes to come.
It drags us, savagely, from that place where we thought we were safe,
where we thought we had it all figured out.....
Those hopes and dreams were what sustained us....
They kept us alive, floating on a magic carpet of ignorance.
They were the fabric of our very existence, that we had woven carefully together, over the years.
Each thread, representing a wish, a long held desire, a belief,
a dream waiting to be awakened into reality.
A tapestry of a life we treasured....A life we thought we knew.
But grief thrusts us, unceremoniously, into the blackness of the unknown
and we are tossed about by the tides of uncertainty...
not knowing when the storm will be over, or if our feet will ever touch firm ground again.
It unhinges us from a reality we thought was firmly secured in place and
hurls us into the dark pit of despair...and loneliness...and isolation.
It robs us of all we held dear.....It takes away the life we once knew.
Those carefree days before grief arrived, have gone now.
Disappearing in the child like innocence that held them together,
lost in the reality that life is not the picture postcard we had carefully painted for ourselves.
Life we discover, has harsh edges...and teeth, that tear into our flesh
hungrily looking to feed on our very soul...if we would allow it.
Gone are the hopes for tomorrow, the dreams we cast into the ocean of our own imagination,
disappearing in one fateful moment in time.
IT WAS NEVER MEANT TO BE LIKE THIS ! ...
A cry of despair, rises out from the depth of my very being, twisting and turning,
making its way out of the darkness, searching for the light it's been denied.
A reply....Soft and gentle....barely a whisper...
BUT WHAT IF IT WAS ALWAYS MEANT TO BE THIS WAY?
The savage claws that gripped my heart are slowly melting now,
like soft velvet snow in the warm embrace of the spring sunlight.
I can breathe. I can take in the sweet scent of the air that my lungs had long lost a taste for.
It refreshes me, like raindrops on bare skin, on a hot dusty, airless day.
I feel a presence...unknown to me before now....standing,
just near enough to be felt... waiting to be recognised and invited in.
I hesitate... She senses this.
'Take my hand' grief says...... She speaks to me in such a gentle, loving way,
I'm completely entranced by her beauty.
Where is the monster that I once thought I knew?
'Take my hand and walk with me awhile,' she invites once again.
'I will show you new hopes and dreams of tomorrow.
We can cast them together, into the kaleidoscope of the cosmos
and watch as they light up the sky, shining the way for others.
For there are others you know.
Many, many others....waking up with hearts gripped in fear of a future unknown.
Come...we will show them there is hope.....there is beauty ...there is love......'

Oftentimes, things felt overwhelming.
My mind would temporarily shut down.
Protecting me perhaps, from overthinking.
So I made a decision to surrender....
or at least that's how it seemed.
Grief told me later,
that surrendering,
is all we can often do at times like these.
It allows the invisible support
(something I was already beginning to sense around me),
to do its work,
to get us over the day to day hurdles.
So I just swam along, on a tide of unknowing,
aware of the storm clouds that hovered nearby.

At that time,
I was unaware that I would not only
be able to weather the storms to come,
but that I would also experience
the wonders of the rainbows that appear,
after the storm clouds have passed.

Grief visited me today
and this time I didn't lock the door
or hide behind the sofa
or put a smile on my face
and pretend she wasn't there.
This time I invited her to introduce herself to me.
I invited her to show me what she had come for.
She in turn, invited me to take a walk
to the waters edge.
And I obediently followed.
The sun had barely made
an impression on the sky
and the moon still cast a slight shadow
on the stillness of the water.
We sat, grief and I and stared out at the horizon.
And in that moment
that sacred moment between
night and day,
grief shared her secrets with me.
She held me while I cried for what I'd lost,
for what I'd not yet understood
and for what I would have to face
in the coming weeks and months.
And she assured me
that I would survive this.
She held me while
I explained to her that
I didn't think I could endure the pain,
that I didn't think I wanted to even try,
that I wasn't strong enough
to bear such sorrow.
And she assured me
that I could ... and that I was.
Then when the crying
and conversation were over,
we sat,
grief and I,
watching the sun rise
and we welcomed in
the dawn of a brand new day.

Searching for peace

Go to the mountains, I thought.
So I went
Dragging my feet
Grumbling at the steep climb
and the rough terrain
that hurt my soles....
Searching.

Go to the ocean, I thought.
So I went and walked for miles
along the seashore
until nighttime fell
and all went dark.
Too dark for searching

Go to the forest, I thought.
So I went and spent
hours among the trees
hugging each one
until my body ached
and my eyes grew tired
Too tired for searching

Go to the river, I thought.
So I went and I sat
and watched the current of the water
playing with driftwood as
the sun sparkled
diamond patterns in white froth
Still searching

"Go into the silence."... a voice whispered
So I went
And there I found peace.

Just a few words...
But they brought with them
a fresh deluge of tears, which breached the fragile sandbanks
of my eyes, cascading in a symmetrical waterfall,
down my cheek bones.
I reached for the nearby chair to steady myself.

Just 3 words... "In loving memory"
on a box that held your ashes.
Ashes, we would later spread like fairy dust
under grand oak trees and weeping willows
that always remind me of the sparklers
my mother would allow me to hold,
as a young child.

Ashes that we'd float down rivers and streams
and watch as they caught the glint of sunbeams,
which made them glisten
with precious diamond particles of you.

Ashes that would sit on countless mantelpieces,
in homes that housed your family and friends,
who'd sit and smile and remember with fondness,
the ways you impacted their lives.... and still do.

Ashes that would travel to exotic places you'd never been to,
yet now hold a part of you for all eternity.

Ashes that we'd sprinkle in the ocean near home,
on your birthday each year,
and laugh at how I'd carried you there,
in a pink tube that once contained
my granddaughter's sweets.

Ashes that would be planted in gardens and flowerbeds,
above which sacred bushes would bloom in summer time,
reminding us of new life amidst our loss.

But all that was to come and today...
Today I wasn't prepared for the box that brought you home to us.
"In loving memory" ...
A box that said just 3 words,
but held so much more.

I may never find the words to express
how much it meant, having you in my life.
Or the words to express how the sound of your laughter
lifted my soul.
Or how your smile lit up every room that you walked into.
Or how your kindness to those who were suffering
touched my heart so deeply.
I may never find the words to express how deeply I grieve ...
Or how painful some days can be.
I may never find the words to thank you
for the time that you gave to those of us on earth
who were fortunate to be called family ...
(We would have liked to have had you for much longer, of course....)
I may never find the words to express the absolute delight you were as a child,
with your mischievous and funny ways.
Or the way words that belonged to a soul who had travelled many lifetimes,
poured from your lips so effortlessly.
I may never find the words to express a love so deep in my heart
that even 'death' can't diminish it,
but only give it wings,
to soar skywards and reach you wherever you are.

We are simply not that powerful

Those of us on this journey with grief,
know and understand that there are circumstances, outside of our control.
I could't save my son.
If it was at all possible....I would have.
We can't control the downward spiral of someone else's mental health
and the pervasive thoughts that are running through their minds.
We can't control the life limiting illnesses
that take over someone else's body.
We can't control the traffic on our roads and prevent accidents.
There are so many things that are outside of our control.
When the question arose in my mind....
Should I have been able to save my child...?
I came to the understanding ....

'I'M SIMPLY NOT THAT POWERFUL'

These words, helped me to put things into perspective and to keep doing so,
whenever negative thoughts arose.
These words helped alleviate the guilt and regret that so often accompany
the grieving process and add to our pain and suffering.

In my conversations with grief, She has taught me that there are indeed
many things I can't control.
She also tells me that importantly, there are certain things
I _can_ control....or at least _learn_ to control.

She tells me I can control how I respond, or react, to outside circumstances,
by the choices I make in the moment.
I can choose to be angry or resentful for example,
or I can choose to be accepting and understanding.

I can choose to follow negative thoughts when they arise,
or I can choose to replace them with more positive ones.

All this information Grief is teaching me, is in turn helping the grieving process.
Each day I am learning acceptance of 'how things are' and not 'how I want them to be'.

This I have found, brings me some degree of peace.

Grief tells me early on,
she can't be fast-tracked
like a parcel...

I find I can't bypass grief, no matter how much I wish I could.
Grief just won't allow it.
She's strict that way.
She tells me there are no shortcuts.
She also assures me she will help me through it.
I have come to trust her, so I believe her when she says
this too shall pass,
when the heaviness of her weighs down on me
and I feel I may buckle under the strain of it all.

She encourages me to feel the emotions as they arise,
however unpleasant they may be.
It helps, she says ... to feel them...
though she doesn't explain why.
She also explains that tears release the pressure
that has built up inside.

I realise that I have forced feelings deep down inside of me
and I know they must be allowed to surface.
Not in one great 'whoosh!'.....
that, grief says, would be too much.

She reminds me to live each day in the full
experience of what it brings.
'Imagine the day is already written', she says,
'and just show up and allow it to support you'.

There is comfort in the words that she speaks.
She tells me some days will bring laughter,
and that I should be OK with that.
Laughter she says can be just as healing as tears....

So I try to allow laughter to enter through the back door of my life,
and not to feel guilty about it....

As I sit at my desk and write, I notice a beautiful heart shape,
appearing in the clouds outside my window,
reminding me of your presence.
My heart opens in gratitude at the signs you send me,
and I feel your love more deeply in this sacred moment in time.

Grief in the beginning, gave expression in different ways...tears...withdrawal...numbness...pain.
A search for some meaning in all of this... A desire to understand.
The "should haves", "could haves", "what if's", knocked on the door of my mind, loudly at times,
but always lurking in the wings.
Through patience and practice, I came to understand the difference between hope and despair...
Came to understand that both, originated in my thoughts.
Then came the wisdom....Direct conversations with my son...
Quiet at first, then louder and more powerful...breaking through the denseness of my grief....
whispering in the silence...in the gaps between thoughts....

WHAT IF ......?

What if there is no death as such ?
What if I'm right here, helping you through this?
What if I hear you when you speak to me?
What if you can survive this?
What if we can learn to communicate in a new way?
What if I see your pain and comfort you when you cry?
What if there was nothing left unsaid?
What if I always knew how much you loved me, and now,
I can see the depth of your love?
What if I watch over you when you sleep?
What if I can send you signs to let you know I'm here?
What if that feather that floated before your eyes was me?
What if that song that played on the radio was me?
What if you stop doubting yourself and start believing?
What if I love seeing you smile, laugh and begin to live life again?
What if we meet every night in your dreams, even if you don't remember?
What if I never miss out on anything, because I'm always with you?
What if I completed my earth journey and now I help from the other side?
What if there are no regrets?
What if grief can sit alongside joy and a passion for living again?
What if I am helping you to heal?
What if you CAN and WILL survive this?
What if what you thought was impossible...is wholly possible?
What if you can expand your consciousness to reach right into my world?
What if our journey together, is only just beginning?
What if life is one continuum?
What if I am living in eternal love and bliss and long to share it with you?
What if you not only survive this....you learn to thrive?
What if these words become an inspiration for others?
These "what if's" that I came to hear time and time again from my son,
pulled me out of the darkness and helped me to understand the bigger picture of eternal life.
He continues to be my greatest teacher.

Something I often told myself in the early days.....

"*If all I did was get dressed this morning,* I'M DOING OK. AND THAT'S MORE THAN ENOUGH"

Be gentle on yourself. You're grieving

Please don't fall into the trap of believing that the deeper we love, the deeper we'll grieve.
Put that way of thinking out of your mind.
Thinking in this way can lead to feelings of guilt if we begin to find enjoyment in life again,
because we somehow feel that we didn't love them enough.
And NOTHING could be further from the truth.

There was a point I came to on this journey,
where I understood that this love I felt for my son while he was in his earthly form,
pales in comparison to the depth of love I feel for him now.
I can't explain why that is, but I expect it has to do with the fact that it's the purest form of love there is.
A love without expectation. A love that flows from soul to soul,
without the physical filter of life in human form.
No expectations of one other...Only love and respect flows between us...

So, in my experience, love doesn't diminish if we begin to live our lives again.
Love only strengthens, and my son encourages me to carry on living life,
and fulfilling this life's purpose, whatever that may be.

The love that pours in from Spirit can heal many deep wounds over time.
Our loved ones are indeed an essential part of our healing journey.
When we consider this, our journey doesn't seem such a lonely one after all.
We have a constant, loving guide and companion by our side,
helping us through any difficulties we may face along the way.

I sometimes have a glimpse of understanding
that I have sacrificed my son's physical form for his spiritual form.
And the question arises,
"If that is the case, what will I do with that, because I sure feel its important
I do something!!"

Each one of us has to choose for ourselves.
For me, I choose to use this "tragedy" as a link to a higher realm.
A deep connection to the Divine, of which my son is not only an integral part,
but a part that is more accessible to me....a personal connection to the Divine.
He has taught me so much already,
and I know there is so much more he has in store for me.

So I begin to embrace this new life with him and allow the deep love and respect we have
for one another to take us on a new journey.
Far from leaving him behind, my son is, and always will be, one step ahead,
encouraging me to live life to the fullest, just as he did in the time he was here.

I know we may not share the same beliefs
as one another .....
I know we may not have been brought up
in the same way,
or walked the same path through life...
I know I may not have suffered the same 'loss'...
in the same way as you...

Yet I feel I know you

as a kindred spirit.

And I honour you,

and the journey

you are on.

Be gentle on yourself,
my friend

Many times, grief has helped me to understand,
that there is so much more to this life,
than meets the human eye.
So much more than our 'human minds' can fathom.

There is a greater force at work here.
Call it The Creator,
God,
The Source,
The Oneness
Great Spirit,
Call it what you will.
We all belong to it
and are connected to it
and therefore
we are all connected to one another.
And therefore,
we will always be connected
to those who have passed
to spirit before us.

This alone, brings me so much peace.

What do you say, to someone who is newly grieving?
People try to say the right thing.
And they are often well meaning in their attempts,
yet they can't take away our pain,
and that is what they are often trying to do,
not understanding that taking away the pain of one who is newly grieving,
is an impossible task.

And in their trying,
they often say things that seem inappropriate to us,
like they are speaking in a foreign language.
Sometimes the words they say can feel like a knife
being plunged into our already broken heart.

I have come to understand that there are no real words one can say,
that will take away the pain of one who is newly grieving,
so it's best not to try.
Actions can often say so much more than words.

Maybe at that particular time,
there is nothing anyone can do for us.
Maybe we just want to be on our own for a while,
knowing there is someone close by,
should we need them.
Or we may want the opportunity to talk about our feelings,
and know we are being listened to,
even if we are not completely understood.

Maybe we just need a loving hand on our shoulder or a warm embrace.
Maybe we just want someone to sit with us in the silence,
but to many people, this feels too uncomfortable.
Most of the time when we are newly grieving,
we don't know what we want from one moment to the next,
so it is difficult for those who wish to comfort us,
to know what's best.

This is something I have come to understand, through experience.

THE FUTILITY OF WORDS.

Your words cannot express the depth of your sorrow,
I know.
They can't express what's in your heart
as you stare helplessly down at me,
a crumpled heap,
lying on the floor
of my own misery.
Your words cannot reach me,
I know.
They can't penetrate the thick skin
of despair.
The dense husk of sorrow that surrounds me
and holds me prisoner,
in its fortress,
a self created protection
enacted by nature,
to cocoon me from shock.
Your words are well meaning
I know.
Yet they sound so trite and out of place,
as they echo around,
in the darkness of my Soul,
like blackbirds hovering overhead,
searching for a place to land,
yet finding none.
Your words are ineffective,
I know.
They cannot reach inside my heart
and douse the fire that is burning there.
They offer just a drop of water,
when what I need is an ocean
to carry me away to the safety
of my own island of grace.

'Leave words for another time',
my heart whispers to yours...
and use your arms to
tell me all you wish to say.'

I have hidden the intensity and depth of my grief from others,
more times than I care to imagine...

Perhaps the one I am hiding it from most,
is myself....

Broken hearted

Yet even in the depth of my grief,
I feel a presence ... encouraging me, with a love so deep ...
pulling me back from the edge of darkness.

The Blackbird sings

It wasn't the blackbird singing that morning that offended me.
For she was only doing what came naturally to her
when a new dawn brought promise
of all the things she held dear.
For me though, there was nothing to sing about,
nothing to delight in
The one thing I held dear was gone.
So why would I sing?
Why would I see the promise in a new dawn?
And besides,
the blackbird, on needing to express herself,
produced a beautiful melody.
A symphony of sounds that woke up the sun from its slumber
and the tree on which she was sitting,
from its restful sleep.
Yet if I were to express myself at this moment,
the sun would certainly retreat
back into the darkness of the night,
startled by a sound that came
from a place it didn't know,
a place it didn't recognise.
For the sun, like the blackbird and the tree,
were things of beauty in this world.
And I was sure,
like I was sure of many things these days
they didn't want their beauty disturbed
by my mournful cries.

I remember clearly,
the last time we hugged.
If I close my eyes,
I can still feel how we held each other
that little bit tighter...
that little bit longer
than we normally would.
I don't think either of us dreamt
it would be the last time
we would see each other...
but I wonder if our souls knew....

Searching for things that would help
with my grief,
I began a gratitude practice.
I had read that being in the energy of gratitude, was helpful,
and in all honesty, I was willing to try anything,
so desperate was I to feel better.
So I began writing in my journal every morning
and every evening,
three things I felt grateful for.
It wasn't easy at first, but I stuck with it
and I soon found, that even though I was grieving,
there were still things I could feel grateful for.
Often, I would write the same thing each day.
I'm grateful for my family and friends who support me...
I'm grateful for a warm blanket to wrap around me...
I'm grateful for the cup of coffee being offered to me this morning...
I'm grateful for the offer of a meal, even though I don't feel like eating...
I'm grateful the sun is shining today...
I'm grateful for a comfortable bed to sleep in...
Simple things, we often take for granted.

Each morning and evening, I wrote in my journal without fail,
even the times I didn't feel like writing,
I still encouraged myself to do so.
And after a while,
I began to feel the benefits of this simple practice.

It is something I still do today...

I told grief that I was having a day off today...
I told her that I was leaving home without her for a change.
I told her that I was exhausted, carrying her around all the time....
She's so heavy!
She looked at me, but didn't say a word...
She just smiled...kindly.
So I packed a small bag with a flask of coffee
and grabbed a banana from the fruit bowl.

Grief can be so draining.
Food doesn't have the same appeal it used to.
I don't want to cook for myself,
so everything is for convenience.
But grief reminds me that if I don't eat properly,
then I will feel worse.
How can I feel worse, I tell her sulkily, though I know she's right.
She usually is.

I throw the bag over my shoulder, grab my keys, and head off,
closing the door with a whoosh behind me.
'There!' I say out loud so grief can hear me...'I'm free!'
And I stride out with purpose.
Back into the normality of everyday living where I once belonged,
but now feel more like a stranger in an unfamiliar play.
An actor who has forgotten which part she's been given.
Could I blend in, like an 'extra'... just for today?

The town is packed with people going about their ordinary lives.
Day-trippers too, there to enjoy the early summer sunshine....
which to be honest, I noticed I wasn't really dressed for.
I was still at the stage of wearing oversized clothes
in an attempt to hide myself from the world.

I watched them, 'the normal people'.... enviously.
They seemed to not have a care in the world.
Can I even remember a time when I felt that carefree?
I put my head down and hurried towards the beach.
It was quieter there.
This part of the beach I'd chosen was seldom crowded.
I liked the fact that I could be by myself, but not completely alone....

cont...

....cont

I could see 'life' going on around me, but I didn't have to participate.
I wasn't anywhere near ready to participate in life!

I sat down on the sand, with my back against the rocks,
took out my flask, and poured some coffee into the small cup.
It was hot, and steam rose into the air,
so I set it down beside me in a dip in the sand, and turned my face toward the sun,
closing my eyes, so I could feel her warmth on my face.
It felt good. It felt good to be out.
It felt good to act normal...
At least as normal as I could pretend to be.

A moment later, I heard the exited cries of a small child. "Look Mummy...Look!"
I opened my eyes instinctively.
The child, a boy around 4 or 5, was holding up a sea shell for his mother to look at.
She bent down to examine it.
She took it gently from him and held it up to the sunlight,
turning it this way and that, like she was gazing upon a priceless artefact.
A big smile floated across her face and I heard her say...
"that's a beautiful shell you've found there."
And in an instant, I was catapulted back to a memory of the past.

A beach holiday when you were little
and loved to hunt for sea shells in the rock pools.
You were always so careful in your searching...
Never wanting to disturb any creatures living there,
just searching for discarded shells to take home to treasure.

I drew my knees up to my chest,
as I felt the all too familiar lump in my throat.
Tears formed in the corner of my eyes and threatened to overflow down my cheeks.

Just then, I felt a warm hand on my shoulder and a gentle squeeze
and I turned to see Grief sitting next to me.
She smiled and held out her hand.
I took it in mine and whispered "thank you".
She smiled back..
"That's OK. You didn't think I'd leave you to struggle alone, did you?"

I never questioned God.
I never questioned why my son died when he did.
God had already whispered in my ear a long time ago,
that there is an order to life.
And that though I may not understand it,
everything was
and always is,
in Divine order.
In a world that felt so chaotic,
those words were of great comfort to me.
So I made them into a mantra
and repeated them often,
to make some sort of
sense, amidst the confusion.

.

Everything is in Divine order...
Everything is in Divine order...
Everything is in Divine order...
Everything is in Divine order...

I am learning to befriend grief.
It has become a daily task,
which begins as soon as I open my eyes in the morning.
Sometimes you may notice grief etched on my face,
like deep lines, chiselled into my cheekbones.
Other times, I may look perfectly normal to you,
and you may even see a smile on my face,
and assume that I'm OK.

But my life is far from the normal.
And I'm far from OK.

But I have decided that I need to <u>befriend</u> grief.
After all, doesn't one know a lot more about a best friend,
than a stranger?

It's taking some effort to get to know her,
but I'm being persistent.
Trouble is, she's so unpredictable...
Not like a best friend at all.

I am always delighted
by the feeling of connectedness to the Spirit realm
and how they show me, they are always listening....

This morning,
I was saying a silent prayer of gratitude
for all the blessings in my life.
I was thanking those in spirit
for all the help and inspiration
they offer me on a daily basis.

As I was standing there, by the window,
I was admiring the beauty of the sky,
the trees, and the birds in the distance,
when the tiniest and brightest of white feathers
came floating past.
I had no doubt it was a sign that my prayers of gratitude were heard.

Learning to trust that connection I have with those across the veil,
who are helping me day to day,
has been such a game changer for me.
I know that my son is now a big part of my 'Spirit Team'
and I also know,
I was fortunate to have had him in his earthy form too,
for a short time.

So much to be thankful for on this journey
called 'Life'.
Today, I feel truly blessed indeed.

No matter how difficult life can get sometimes,
the 'human spirit' has an enormous capacity
for lifting itself up out of the darkness.
This has been my own personal experience,
and what I've come to understand,
from the experiences of those I've read about
and those I've personally encountered on this journey with grief.

There is something so much MORE to us,
that we don't fully understand (yet instinctively know),
that guides us through life's most difficult challenges.

Learning to embrace and LOVE this part of ourselves
is one of the many things Grief has taught me.
This part of us, I believe,
is the part that has always been with us,
and can never leave us,
It is the part that survives 'physical death'.
Call it our Essence, our Soul, or our Spirit,
it is the part of us that is capable of much, much more
than our limited 'human self'.

Learning to live from this part,
has helped me to move through deep grief towards healing.
This part of me accepts that there is no death...
we simply transform.
This part of me knows that I can withstand the greatest of storms
and yet still feel a deep peace within.

This part of me is always there and _has_ always been there.
A trusted friend, offering a soft place to land.

I honour and love this part of myself every day
and I honour Grief for showing me what is possible.

Sometimes, I go out at night and stare up at the stars,
wondering where you are.
Then I feel your presence beside me,
and hear you whispering...
reminding me,
that you are right here.

Our loved ones see our struggles...

I watch you from the other side.
I see you bending down, to pick up the pieces
of your broken heart
with hands that are so sore
from washing....lots of washing...
A way to keep busy...I know.

I watch you from the other side...
Painting on a smile in the bathroom mirror,
so others, when they see you,
will think you're OK...
that you're getting there..
that you're doing well...
'under the circumstances', they say.

I watch you from the other side...
As you struggle with your keys
with fingers that seem to have lost their grip
and a mind that you fear
is losing its grip on reality...

I watch you from the other side...
and how you fight with every ounce of
strength that you've got,
to function every day....not because you want to,
but because however much you may not want it to
...life must go on.

I watch you from the other side
And I am so very proud of you.
I'm in awe of all that you do.

And I love you with every breath you take....
And I want you to know, I am beside you ...
every brave and difficult step that you make.

<u>Give yourself permission to rest.</u>

If your body is feeling weary,
and you are struggling to face the day,
remember that spark inside of you,
that's always there....lighting your way.
This spark is one of wisdom,
of hope and strength and love...
This spark is the light of Divinity,
that connects you with heaven above.
So just settle yourself on your sofa,
wrap yourself up in a blanket and stay...
Let your mind be at rest,
let your heart bring you peace,
you've done more than enough for one day.

I wish I'd captured a photo of it for my collection,
but images in the clouds disappear so quickly.
And, as you so often remind me,
I need to learn to appreciate and enjoy things in the moment.
I'd heard your encouragement to watch the skies for a sign,
a few days before,
and I'd been enjoying watching the various cloud formations
and the way the colours of the early morning sunrise
changed each day,
like an invisible hand was free-painting it for all to enjoy.
So while sitting at my desk writing,
I glanced out of the window
and there was a perfectly shaped pair of headphones,
the type you used to wear when you were listening to music
or playing the decks.
Your blue headphones, are one of the few possessions I have of yours.
You always told me how much music meant to you.
So I thank you for this unique sign in the clouds,
and for letting me know you are always with me as I write.

Sometimes when we are grieving,
we can feel cast adrift, like we are roaming
in the wilderness,
where there are no signposts or information points.
The times I have felt like this,
I've taken it as a sign to do some searching of my own.
I'm assured, after many years,
that there is something I need to uncover
for myself and that what I find, will hold value for me.
Needing to take an active part in my
healing journey has opened many new doors.
I know instinctively that I am being guided.
We all are.
But sometimes, we need to feel cast adrift,
to surrender, and allow ourselves to be guided.
Sitting daily, in quiet meditation,
can help us through this wilderness
and bring much wisdom
to the soul that is searching for truth.

We may have been taught things by our parents,
by society, our culture, our religion etc.
about what happens after 'death'.
But when we experience the 'death' of someone close to us,
we may feel the need to challenge the beliefs
we have adopted and do some research for ourselves.

There is undeniable evidence out there,
of the continuation of life after physical death....
lots of it!
Science is slowly catching up with what
our ancestors have always known....
There is no 'death' as we know it,
only a continuation of life.

So we may find ourselves needing to take down the walls of belief,
that were erected for us,
as we open ourselves up
to a whole new way of looking at things.
Then, a world beyond the five senses
will slowly make itself known to us...

A world where our loved ones dwell.

I came to value the importance,
of taking long walks in nature,
as a way to soothe my weary soul

Often, when we are grieving,
things that would have normally brought us joy,
don't touch us as they once did.
It's as if a veil has been dropped, between us and life itself.
Our eyes, our ears and our other senses too,
no longer seem able to bear witness to what surrounds us.
We are as if in a bubble.

From my own experience, I believe we are protected in the early days,
from feeling the full force of our loss...
lest it destroy us with its intensity.
We can remain there, cut off from the world for quite some time.
And when we feel ready or when we feel we need to, or have to emerge,
it can be a difficult integration back into normal everyday life.
For a while, things don't appear the same.
Sounds can seem louder and colours seem dimmed,
as if our senses took their leave, and have not quite returned.
I remember I couldn't spend much time in large grocery stores.
The sounds were too loud,
the people seemed much too hectic in their movements
and the sheer vastness of the stores,
made me want to retreat back to the safety of my four walls.
I feel that this is common among those of us who are grieving,
yet how to deal with it became a question I needed answering
and I knew it was something I would have to work out for myself.

So I began with limiting my visits to places where there were lots of people and noise.
I began going into smaller shops for my groceries,
and at times I knew, would be less busy.
I began taking long walks in parks and around the lake near home,
where the sight and fragrance of
the fresh air and wild flowers, comforted my senses.
I lived near the coast, so I went there too, and allowed
the sound of the ocean waves, to soothe and relax me.
I found that being out in nature, helped and I found much clarity,
on these 'solitary walks'.
I knew I wasn't completely alone during these times.
I knew my son was with me every step of the way.... I'd asked him to be.
I knew, even though in the early days I couldn't feel his presence all that much,
I knew instinctively he was there beside me.
So these walks in nature, served to gently soothe me back to life.

I came to recognise, that not everyone understood the depth of pain
that accompanies grief.

In the beginning,
I thought it would be obvious to people.
My son was dead...therefore, I was in immense pain.
Yet I found that the pain of grief is deeply personal
and no-one could feel the pain I was feeling,
therefore they couldn't fully understand how I felt.
Others, who had suffered a similar loss, could certainly empathise,
and attest to the fact that the pain is often unbearable,
but no one could feel MY pain.

I also came to discover, that some people expect the one who is grieving,
to recover more quickly than they are able.
Maybe people have reasons of their own, for wanting this to be the case,
but there is no time frame for grief.
Everyone should be allowed to have the time and the space,
to grieve in their own way.

Certainly grief can become 'complicated' for some.
I'd read about complicated grief,
when a heightened state of mourning prevents the healing process from occurring.
But I knew I wanted to heal.
I knew I not only wanted to survive the death of my son...I wanted to thrive too.
I wanted to enjoy life again, in the future.
I instinctively knew this was possible.
I had two grandparents who had lost children, to draw strength from.

But I also knew that it would take time......
That the process of grieving is a 'sacred act' and deeply personal.
I knew I would be up some days and down the next.
I knew that I,
like grief itself, would be unpredictable.

I hoped that the people around me would understand that,
.....and make allowances for me.
I also hoped that they would understand
that I would not be the same person I was before.....

Excuse me if I seem insensitive
and a bit abrupt today.
Excuse me if my words seem a little bit harsh,
and not what you expect me to say.
Sometimes your troubles seem trivial,
and I struggle to sympathise
When the weight of grief I carry around,
feels so colossal in size

Things that you mention that bother you,
seem so insignificant now, to me,
I don't have the same perspective these days,
to see things the way that you see.

The neighbour playing loud music,
the cost of eggs, bacon and bread,
the dog that keeps barking up the street,
it all goes over my head.

When grief is overwhelming,
understand my need to step back.
I have to protect myself from falling,
and disappearing down the cracks.

I know you often fail to notice,
but my struggle is very real,
it takes so much of my inner strength,
to hold it together and heal.

So excuse me if I seem insensitive,
or sound a bit harsh today,
walk a mile in these shoes of mine,
and your troubles may just fade away".

I have scars.
I have earned them on the battlefield of life....
as I fought with reality and pain.
I earned them when I fought to find meaning
in a world without you in it.
I earned them when I fought with all my might,
to get back up,
when the turbulent storms of grief,
knocked me off my feet with lightening force,
and rendered me immobile.
I earned them by getting up each morning,
not knowing what pain the day may bring,
what sorrow it may entail,
what difficulties my new reality would have me face.
I have scars.
I earned them on the battlefield of life.
And I am noticing
that these scars are forming
an intricate pattern,
an 'original' design,
one that pays homage to my suffering and pain.
One that says,
keep going...
Your scars are a beautiful reminder
of all the love that's in your heart.

This is an practice that I do often.
I began it quite early on in my journey.
I call it a 'mini retreat for the mind'.

Doing this exercise, or practice,
gives yourself the gift of a 5 minute retreat
from all the mental chatter that so often disturbs our minds.
Have a notebook, or your grief journal to hand.
Begin by sitting quietly.
You may want some soft music, playing in the background.

Close your eyes and say the following words.

"I feel truly blessed by your presence"

Feel into these words.
Say them over a few times, out-loud if possible.

Now open your eyes and your journal
and write whatever comes to mind.
You may be pleasantly surprised.

Other phrases I use are...
"It's good to know you're never more than a thought away from me".

Or you may have a particular question you may wish to ask your loved one.

This form of inspired writing has helped me a great deal in my grief.

Rejoining life, can be a struggle at first.
Take your time.
Meander a while.
All routes you take toward healing,
are valuable.

I shielded my eyes against the sunlight I felt had deserted me,
yet had been there all along,
waiting....beyond the front door.
The darkness that had
enfolded me in its grasp, for how long,
I'm unsure,
retreated.
For a moment, I felt free
Freer than I had done, in a long time.
As my gaze rested on the landscape,
it felt unfamiliar to my
weary eyes.
How long since I had wandered
down country lanes,
marvelling at the speed in which
the hedgerows grow in summer time ?
Or felt the warmth of the midday sun,
coaxing the butterflies from
the safety of their cocoon
to rise on wings anew ?
Yet here I stood
on unsteady legs
that had spent far too long
hidden under the cover of
bedclothes, or warm fleece blankets that
draped the backs of sofas...
adding colour to an otherwise
sombre room.
To step out would be to
admit I was recovering
that I was doing OK
that 'this'
this grief that had held me captive for so long,
was somehow over.
But I knew it wasn't.
It was only just beginning.
And with all the strength I could lend to my shaky legs,
I stepped over the threshold
and the sunlight gave me back my wings.

Living without the physical presence of someone we love,
isn't easy, but we do the best we can.
Some survive by keeping themselves busy,
for fear of falling into the blackness of depression they know is never far away.
Some discover a spiritual path they never would have gone down before.
Some survive by throwing themselves into raising money for charities,
or raising awareness for a cause, close to their loved one's heart.
Some survive by putting on a brave face and
putting one foot in-front of the other,
while quietly marking off the days.

Whichever way we manage our 'loss',
we can rest assured,
that we will see our loved ones again.
And what a glorious reunion it will be.

It takes time to learn how to adjust and live alongside grief.
So we need to be gentle with ourselves.
Just as life is a journey...
Grief is also a journey.... destination unknown.
Grief can open many spiritual doors
and take us to places we would never have gone 'before'.
Would we trade this to have our loved ones back beside us, happy and healthy?
Of course we would,
but as that's not possible, we can choose perhaps,
to grow through this grief of ours
and allow her to teach us all there is to know
about everlasting life....

'Grief is just love with no place to go.'
I have seen these words written many times,
and have never understood, or resonated with them.
So early on in my journey, I questioned them.

In my heart, I knew that the love we have, reaches those on 'the other side'.
Love as I have come to know it, is an energy that cannot be contained,
therefore it HAS to go somewhere.
Maybe I'm being a bit pedantic I thought,
but grief HAS to be so much more than 'love with no place to go'.

So in my conversations with Grief I told her...
I want my love to continue to flow... I want it to continue to be an expression
of how I feel towards my son in spirit ...
I want to continue to LOVE in all ways.
I want love to flow outwards.....and inwards.
I told Grief that I _feel_ the love from those in Spirit who have left 'the play of life',
but still stand 'off stage,' encouraging us ...
and I want them to feel the love I am sending them, too."

Grief listened, as she always does....
Then she assured me that my love is _always_ felt by those I'm attached to.
"That's what holds you together"....Grief said,
"this exchange of energy...
back and forth...
in a never ending circle.
It is _meant_ to be this way".

And I came to realise, that love is what holds the parts of me together also,
when I feel I'm falling apart.
Love never dies... It doesn't diminish.
Maybe it increases by being shared.
Like ripples on a pond....it flows out.
Love cannot be contained...
It must flow....
Grief is an expression of love, yes.....
But in its expression _as_ love, it has a place to go....
It goes out and reaches our loved ones in spirit.
This is what Grief has taught me....

Many times on this journey and in my conversations with grief,
I have questioned where I am going.
If I'm walking along this path,
what is my destination?
Am I travelling from a state of grief to a state of non-grief?
Should I be doing something to hasten my journey?
Should I be looking for a shortcut perhaps?
Do I really <u>need</u> to get to the end quicker?
Is there indeed, an end to grief?

I'm not sure there is a 'right answer'
to any of these questions that often crop up in my mind.

I know grief is painful.
I know that sometimes I desperately want to feel "normal" again.
I know that often I'm afraid if I break down, I'll never get back up again.
I imagine my family would feel better if they think I'm doing OK
Sometimes I even believe, I SHOULD be doing better

So many questions keep coming up....just as grief keeps coming up.
They seem to ride in tandem with one another.
So I decide to stop trying so hard, to 'go' anywhere
and decide it's better for me to get still.
I decide to experience everything that arises in the moment.

I don't always succeed of course.
But I try and keep on trying.
I know how important it is for me, not to shortcut this grief of mine,
but to give it the expression it needs.

And as I began to do this more and more,
I began to hear my son's words encouraging me......
It's okay to feel sad, you know.
But remember, it's also okay for you to feel happy.
I know you miss me desperately at times
and sometimes you worry that you are going to remain stuck
in this never-ending cycle of grief.
But I want to reassure you that things can and will change.
It's important that you are gentle with yourself.
When one is grieving, self-love becomes essential.

cont....

cont....

Remember too, that it's okay to visit past memories that make you smile .
We in spirit, love to see our loved ones smile,
though we appreciate how difficult this can be for you sometimes.

****

Throughout this journey,
Grief keeps reminding me not to be afraid to feel the whole range of emotions as they arise.
Pleasant or unpleasant, sooner or later all feelings and emotions change, she says.

Grief has become a part of my life.....
Losing someone we love, is something most of us will experience at some point in our lives.
Many of us will experience deep grief, several times over.
Some losses run very deep and it is important to allow them room to breathe.
This is how we heal, by making time for and giving space to the grieving process.

And I have come to know that we CAN heal, even if we never thought we could...or would.
It is innate within us to heal.
The body heals a cut all by itself.
It knows how to do it.
And I trust it knows how to heal a broken heart, too.
So I've been letting it heal my heart for a while now.
I've been letting it do what it needs to do.
I've been giving it space to do that.
And that's OK.
It's all OK.
Nothing is 'not OK' as far as grieving is concerned.
Follow your heart, and it will let you know whether to laugh, or cry, or be silent.
It will let you know if it wants to be in company, or wants to be alone.
Do this your own way...It's _your_ grief.
Others may give advice and say what they are doing,
and if it resonates with you, give it a try.
But there is no right or wrong way to grieve.....
Give yourself permission to do it your way.
And your way may change as time goes by.
I know mine has.

Learn to pay attention to what your heart is telling you.
Learn to listen to, and trust it.
Your loved one is very much entwined in that heart of yours.

And they are an important part of this journey you are on.

Guilt and Regret....

"Stop with the guilt already"! I hear you say.
"No, you couldn't have saved me
....you're simply not that powerful!
No you couldn't have done more than you did.
You did all that you knew how, at the time.
I see that now.
I see all of it.
My life was my own, to do with as I chose.
My choices,
my mistakes....
My wins,
my losses...
My triumphs,
my disasters...
All Mine!
So stop with the guilt already"!

Underneath the many layers, that living in this world
with all its demands and challenges puts on us,
my son reminds me that we are all 'beautiful souls'.
He reminds me that we are all strong enough to weather the darkest of storms
because we are all connected to spirit.
Indeed we are.... all spirit.
It may sound strange to some,
when I say that it's a privilege to have my son in spirit,
yet this is how it sometimes feels after almost 4 years.
At other times, I look at his beautiful face in a photograph
and cry like the rain,
wishing he was back at my side...
in person...in the flesh.

These "Dances with Dan" as I call them,
force me to see life through a different lens....
The lens of the soul.
Through this lens I see reality as it truly is....
No separation
No coming or going
No beginning or end.
Just a continuation of a love story that began a long time ago
A love story that has many chapters in a book that has no end.

This is what my son's transition has taught me....
and keeps teaching me.
And the more I know, the more I realise
there's still so much to learn....
to experience,
in this crazy, magical and mysterious world that I was thrust into.

And some days when I wake now,
I am beginning to feel the delicate stirrings of hope,
birthing life into me, once again.

Losing a child to addiction, can be complicated.
Guilt and regret often rear their ugly head,
and become entangled in our grief, if we aren't mindful.
And these complex emotions, can cause us to suffer greatly, on top of everything else.

Guilt and regret serve no purpose, my son tells me.
Each is an insidious energy, which eats away at, and erodes the very fabric of our being.
Yet, there have been, and still are, many times when guilt sneaks into my awareness
and threatens to drag me down into that black hole with no end to its depth.
And sometimes, I have to fight hard to make my way back up to the surface.

To understand guilt fully, we would each need to define it for ourselves.
It's too simple to just say...I feel guilty that I didn't do this or that, or I didn't do enough.
We need to dig deeper to see where the emotion or feeling of guilt is coming from.
It's a deep dive into ourselves and often it's too painful, so we don't go there.
Yet I have found that I needed to and therefore wanted to go there in order to heal.
Looking at the past, when the past is often painful, isn't easy.
I still hesitate at the doorway and stare down into the darkness
and wonder if I am brave enough.
If I'm not brave enough in that moment,
I'm kind enough to myself, to save the 'looking' for another day.
This isn't a one time fix all .... it's a process that may need repeating many times.

What we need to consider,
besides what we feel we could have, or should have done,
is what we DID do...
over and over and over again.
How much responsibility we shouldered...
How much pain and worry and stress we carried...
How much peace and joy of life, we lost along the way.
We couldn't blame our loved one.
Nobody sets out to become addicted and the illness of addiction
is mis-understood by most people, myself included.
Very often I had to hide from the truth, because the truth was far too painful to face.
The very real possibility of getting 'that phone-call', haunted me for many years,
as anyone who has walked this path with a loved one, will know, all too well.
We know they aren't intentionally causing us pain and worry,
yet the pain and worry is present, all the same.
In our 'not wanting them to suffer', we also suffered greatly.
We were powerless to change things.

cont...

...cont

Helping them, may have served to make us feel better at the time.
We could convince ourselves we were doing the right thing.
but it was never a solution to the 'problem'....
We weren't the ones holding the power .... And neither were they.

Some people can and do recover from addictions, and I am always heartened
when I read the stories of those who managed it.
But many, many others can't and those that try and fail, over and over again,
often feel great shame, disillusionment, and isolation, which adds to their struggle.
We who have travelled this path, have suffered more than enough.
Living with a loved one suffering from addiction, is one of life's harshest lessons.
And the same goes for the one suffering the addiction.

I now choose to be kind to myself. Not only because I know Dan would want that
for me, but because I want it for myself too. I can't allow guilt or regret to bring me down.
I visit it when I am brave enough and I challenge it with all the good I did.
I challenge it with how much I loved him, with how many times I tried and failed to
change things. I challenge it with how brave I was and still am.
Now is not the time to allow guilt to taint the beautiful memories I have of my child....
there will never be time for that.
Addiction has robbed us both of so much time already.

I always hoped and prayed that the outcome would turn out differently than it did,
but since Dan's death, I have come to understand, that for some of us,
the paths we take in life, are paths that were planned long before we came here.
I'd never contemplated, or even heard about 'soul planning' before Dan died,
but he led me to a book which changed all of that for me.
He helped me to understand that NOTHING I did, could have kept him from leaving.
It was all decided long before he took human form.
And when I look back on conversations we had, I can see things more clearly.
He always said he'd never grow old.
I used to worry about that, but I pushed it to the back of my mind.
If this is the first time you are hearing of 'soul plans', and it doesn't resonate with you,
then please dismiss it... In truth, I don't think we all make such plans.
If it's the first time you are hearing of it and it does resonate with you, then look it up.
I know my son doesn't exist in the darkness any longer.
I know his struggles have ended.
His Spirit dwells in the light.
He tells me that's where I will find him.
So I work hard at dissolving the guilt I carry...... So I can stay in the light...

Our Place

I carved out a special place in my home.
I call it my sanctuary.
There is a small table next to a comfortable chair,
on which I placed a photograph of you,
alongside a candle which I light each day.
This space that I created, I visit often.
It has become imbued with the energy of you.
Here, I sit and feel close to you.
Here, I meditate.
Here I talk with you about my day.
Here I ask you questions
and 'scribe' your answers in my journal.
Here,
in this sacred space I have created,
I feel an inner peace
and a connection to all that is.

I have found, that creating a special place in the home, or maybe in the garden,
where you can sit with your loved one and share your thoughts and feelings with them,
is very comforting and healing.

"Why don't you come and sit with me awhile?"
are words I often hear from my son.
He encourages me to take time out to 'be' with him.
He encourages me to share my feelings, my worries, my joys, my accomplishments.
When I take the time to sit and talk with him,
I feel a joy within my heart and my day seems to flow better.
Often, I will write in my journal and sometimes
I will talk outloud, or in my mind.
It doesn't seem to matter which mode of communication I choose.
He's always there to listen.

Often, all we want is to be heard, yet those close to us may find it hard to 'just listen'....
as they want to fix things for us.
They assume we are sad, or will get sad if we talk about our loved one.
I have come to recognise this in people over the years.
There's no judgement of them here, just an understanding that they may not
have the 'ability' to fully understand.
I know my son is always available to listen.
Our loved ones across the veil, fully understand.
They embrace us in our joy as well as our sorrow.
They invite us to talk with them...
So that's what I do.
I talk....he listens.
Sometimes he gives advice.
More often he just wraps me in a warm feeling of love.
That feeling of love, acts like a healing balm....

Changing...Becoming...Embracing a new perspective.

People around us often find it difficult to relate to us,
after the passing of a loved one.
They may yearn for the 'old you'.
The familiar you... the person you used to be....
But 'that one' is gone...Changed....We are simply not the same.
And this, is what they often find difficult.
People have a habit of seeking out the familiar.
It makes us feel safe.
But in truth, nothing ever stays the same
and those of us who are grieving, understand this more than most.
Having someone we love return home before us....how can we not be changed?
We look at life through a different lens now...
A whole new perspective opens and slowly comes into view.
We can't go back.
And if we try...try to be the same, do the same things,
it all seems so foreign to us.
Life changes us. It is always changing us.
For isn't that the purpose of life?
Some changes are small, inconsequential even.
Yet from each small change, a new person emerges.
The transition of someone you love dearly,
is by no means a small change.
It is huge! Colossal!
The person than emerges from the embers,
is nothing like the one that went into the flames.
This person, if allowed to, will have a greater understanding of life.
A greater understanding of pain and how to move through it.
A greater understanding and more compassion for those who are suffering.
A greater understanding that 'death' does not mean the end of life...
but a doorway to another dimension,
far greater than the one we exist in at present.
This person may also come to understand that 'birth' wasn't the beginning,
but a continuation of the Soul's journey from one life to the next.
They may begin to understand that each lifetime is finite in regard to its length,
yet even the shortest life can have a profound impact and
potential for growth for the Soul concerned,
and also for those whose lives they touch by their presence.

cont....

cont.....

As a mother of a child in spirit, I often stare off into space...
Gaze at a beautiful sunset for longer than usual....
stop to smell the flowers and appreciate their incredible beauty.
I will most likely notice a penny on the sidewalk,
or a feather in my path that others miss.
I may notice the way the raindrops fall on the window pane,
and trace the trail they leave behind, with my fingertip.
I may notice the buds on the tree outside my window
and how they open up slowly each day when caressed
by the warmth of the morning sun.
I may notice the birdsong is more beautiful than I ever believed it to be.
That the rolling waves of the ocean have their own unique melody that only I can hear.
I may find I enjoy walking barefoot on the grass
and laying under a tree for hours,
watching the clouds paint pictures in the sky.
For me, the sky has become a canvas,
a way for spirit to communicate with those of us on earth, who understand.
This person I was, the person who went into the fire,
is not the same person who emerged.
Some of those around me, may yearn to have that old version back.
Indeed, I may at times, yearn for that old version of myself too.
But grief tells me.....that given time and space and understanding,
this new person that is emerging,
may just have a gift to offer the world.

So don't let others change you.
Don't let them tug at you to bring that 'old version' of you back.
Don't let them tell you what you should or shouldn't do, or think, or feel.
Embrace who you are now.... And who you are becoming.
You have the light of your loved one burning brightly inside of you.
You see the world through new eyes.
Maybe we, who have been through this fire,
have walked these hot coals for a reason.
Maybe we are here to bring more light and understanding into the world.
And if those around us can't see that yet....
Give them time...Give them patience, understanding, compassion. Give them love.
But stand firm.
Do it from your new perspective.
Do it from the person you now know yourself to be.
Do it for you...for your loved one....for the world.

Searching

I searched for your face in the clouds today.
I do that sometimes, when I'm out and about
and the sky is blue,
with billowing white clouds
making a perfect canvas for you to paint on.

I saw you once...a few years back.
On the anniversary of your 'death'.

I was sitting on the grass on a warm spring day.
Something.... (you) nudged me to look up.

And there was your face!
It took me by surprise
and I didn't dare reach for my phone
to take a picture.
I didn't want to take my eyes off you,
in case you drifted away..... Which of course you did.

I didn't see you today.

But I'll search again tomorrow.

Searching....Again

My poor, weak, fragile self has taken a battering.
I know I've largely been ignoring her.
My attention is elsewhere.
It's out in the ether, searching for you.

I know I have to come back down soon....but.
Down there is where the pain of real life is.
Down there is where life moves on and I stand still,
stuck to the spot from which you vanished.
Down there is where other people dance and sing and
live their lives with not a care in the world.

Where is my carefree life?
Where is the beat of my drum that birthed me in to being?
Where is my own unique rhythm so I can dance and sing?
Gone...
So I'll float a while longer.
The cosmos is so much larger than I expected,
so I may be here for quite some time.
and there's no guarantee of finding you.

Are you hiding from me?
Are you on another level,
a level I can't reach with the weight of this human body
and such a heavy heart?
I've lost 15 pounds since you left.
Will this help me to float higher?
Since losing you, there seems so much less of me to lose.
Is that a light I see in the distance?
It looks brighter than the stars and planets I've just passed by.
There's a moment when my heavy heart feels lighter
and almost skips a beat.

Perhaps tonight is the night I find you in my dreams...

Each and every one of us has the ability
to connect with the Divine light of our loved one.
The wisdom that we find there is priceless.
This wisdom, this love, this strength, this support,
this light of theirs,
contains everything we need
(and will ever need),
to carry us through any and all of the difficulties we face.
If we can remember this,
it may just help us endure the lightening storms of grief when they come.
Just know, that wherever you are on your journey,
the connection is and always will be there.
Think of it as an invisible thread that connects the both of you together,
and give it a gentle tug now and then, to see what happens....

In daily life, when someone we love has come for a visit,
or maybe we have travelled to visit them and returned home,
it is natural to miss their company for a while.
That closeness, brought on when two people are physically together,
is a unique experience that is often taken for granted,
especially if loved ones live close by and we see them regularly.
But if there is a great distance between us,
and we don't get to see them very often,
for a while after we've parted company,
it can feel like they are a million miles away.
Phone-calls are precious,
but nothing can compare with that physical closeness
that two human beings share
when they are together.

This is what we miss when a loved one returns home before us.
We miss that physical bonding......
Those hugs....
Especially those hugs......
And we also miss those precious phone-calls or text messages.

If I had to describe 'loss' in simple terms,
it would be the loss of the ability to do what comes most naturally to us.
To hug one another physically and to speak to one another,
be it face to face, or over the phone.

We have to adapt to a new way of being.
Adapt to a new.... (and in the beginning), unfamiliar relationship with our loved ones,
who now exist in spirit form.
But we can still HAVE a relationship with them,
and this is important to know.
We will need to work at it,
especially in the beginning when we are trying things out,
to see what works for the both of us.
But the rewards a relationship with those in spirit brings, can be life-changing
for those who are grieving.

That being said....
I will ALWAYS miss those wonderful hugs from my beautiful son and my dear mother.

Grief gives me gentle reminders and encouragement. She says....

Take Small Steps Every Day

Grief...
My most humblest of teachers
My constant companion
My confidant
My friend

Yes, it has taken me quite some time to appreciate your worth.
To be willing to embrace you...instead of pushing you away.
To let you into my heart, instead of holding you at arms length,
or hiding in the shadows hoping you wouldn't find me there...
with tears streaming down my face.

Now you have helped me understand.
Now you have cleaned the lens of my vision
enough for me to gaze upon your beauty.
Now I see what an exquisite treasure you are.
A friend I never knew I had.
A teacher..a master of the highest order.

You have come to guide me.
Back to my true self
My true essence
My truth
THE Truth...
You have come to rescue me
from the battlefield of my own mind
which can be a dangerous and frightening place.

I'm still a toddler taking baby steps beside you.
I'm still apt to wobble...to fall.
Yet I know now...with certainty,
that you are here to catch me if and when I do.
And you will put me back together again
if I should ever fall apart...which I will....
Many times...
Grief
My constant companion
My friend...
Thank you...

Grief came silently today,
like patters of raindrops on my heart.
Soft and gentle I felt her presence
I closed my eyes and focused on my breathing
slowly...deliberately.

I've learnt to do this.

'Not here', I silently plead.
I was sitting at my favourite pavement cafe
and it was extremely busy.
But grief doesn't wait for the perfect time.
Grief moves to her own agenda.
She doesn't wait for a convenient time to show up.
She creeps up unexpectedly
and catches you unaware.

I've learnt this too.

Mostly I can breathe through it
when the waves are just ripples.
Thankfully, today they are ripples,
like the waves on the ocean in front of me.
So I reach for my sunglasses
to hide my tears
and carry on sipping my coffee....

I had been reading a lot about signs from our loved ones in spirit.
Dan had already sent me quite a few, but I was always eager for more.
I'd been reading that it's possible to ask for a specific sign,
so I set about trying it out.
I closed my eyes, quietened my thoughts and said,
OK Dan, what sign shall we choose.
Quick as a flash, I heard the word kingfisher.
I felt myself protesting at once.
There's no chance of me seeing a kingfisher around here, I said.
Can't we choose something else?
It seemed unfair to change such a definite word though,
so I trusted that I would be sent a kingfisher in some shape or form,
understanding that it didn't have to be the actual bird,
but could be a photograph,
or a representation of a kingfisher, too.

The following morning, I set off on a planned day out to the country gardens .
It had become a favourite place of mine
and I always felt replenished and rejuvenated after being out in nature.
It was a journey of around 25 miles through country lanes to get there
and about halfway, I came across a sign saying ...
'Road ahead closed'.
I hoped that I would be able to get through somehow,
but when I travelled a few miles further,
the road was indeed closed and a detour was in place.
This meant a very long way around and as I was working later, I didn't really have time.

I was disappointed that my plans had been thwarted,
and turning my car around, decided somewhat begrudgingly,
to go into the market town to have a coffee
and wander around the shops instead.
I parked up and made my way towards a favourite cafe of mine,
passing a health food store on the way. Ah, I thought...I need toothpaste.
I might as well get it now that I'm here.
I went in and asked where the toothpaste was and the assistant pointed me in the
right direction. I picked up a tube of toothpaste to check the price,
and a big beaming smile lit up my face!
There on the toothpaste tube was a picture of....You guessed it!
A KINGFISHER
It took a road block and thwarted plans, for Dan to bring my sign to me,
but I couldn't have been happier or more grateful!

Our loved ones in spirit
will always occupy
that special place,
right in the centre
of our heart.
It's as though that place
was already carved out,
... just for them...

Grief told me I would have to dig deep
to discover the place within myself
where all knowledge dwelt.
Not the knowledge one learns at school, or university,
but the knowledge that resides deep within us all.
Knowledge that resides in those unexplored places,
that many will never have cause to visit.
Yet for me, the time had come to venture there.
To explore with an unencumbered mind
free of judgement, free of conditioning,
free of other people's opinions and voices of right and wrong.
I knew I had to discover that place for myself.
The place within, where my true power lay.
And even though I knew I had to venture alone,
I also knew that I may need, and was willing to accept guidance,
from those who had travelled that way before me.
Pilgrims who had forged the path with footprints of dedication and faith,
forging a trail, for those who were to follow.
And Grief led me gently along.
Along a path, invisible until now,
yet always there,
silently waiting
for a time to reveal itself.
And the time for me was now.
As I sat in the ominous silence
that had mysteriously arisen,
I sat.
I sat for guidance.
I sat to remember.
I sat to be shown the way
by a presence that has always been with me,
unseen, unfelt,
unneeded....
until now.

Sometimes I can carry grief around
and hardly know
she's there.
Other times,
she's like one of those suitcases
you see at the airport carousel,
stamped with a red caution label saying....

HEAVY !

Caution
Baggage
Contains
GRIEF

My Darling Heart

Oh my darling beating heart.
Oh how I honour you for keeping on beating
when you could so easily have stopped....
to have given up trying to sustain a body that
wanted to melt into the comfort of non-existence
...and would easily have done so, if you had just authored it.

Oh my darling beating heart,
how you have pulled me back time and time again,
from the mire of my own imagination,
where death seems so much more inviting than life,
where promises are kept ...not broken,
where life is devoid of gut-wrenching pain.

Oh my darling beating heart,
how I love to feel your gentleness,
your radiance,
your reliability,
soothing me back into the light,
serenading me back into awareness
back into my own being,
where I can grow and glow
in the moonlight of your breath.

Oh my darling beating heart.
I feel your gentle kiss of encouragement
as I awaken each day
to a new morn that offers
so much hope,
so much beauty,
so much love.

Oh my darling heart...
Thank you for continuing to
create our own sweet music with the
strong, steady beat of your faithful drum,
to guide me through all of this pain
and to connect me once more,
to the rhythm of my very own dance with life.

*A lifetime, however brief or long, holds much wisdom and many miracles for all those who witness it.
We are all so beautifully connected in love...* ♡

Dances with Dan: Embracing Grief

Grief can last a whole lifetime.....
Sympathy and understanding it seems, has an expiry date.
This has been my experience since my son's passing, as well as what
I've heard from others on the same path.
People lead such busy lives....and most have struggles of their own.
So I came to realise that I can't always depend on the support of others when I need it.

I appreciate that this is MY journey, and I must learn to walk it as best I can.
I no longer question the struggles placed before me,
and I trust fully in the bigger picture, even though I don't know the fullness of it,
only that there are hidden treasures that are mine to discover.

I know I'm never alone on this journey,
and knowing this has been fundamental in how I've coped with and grown
from walking through this fire of grief.

I have been encouraged to develop a deeper relationship with my son in spirit,
and he is the one who provides the strength and support I need,
when I need it....and the wisdom, too,
to understand this path I am now on and how to walk it with grace.

The passing of someone we dearly love calls on us to develop resilience
and a deeper understanding of human nature.

I find I have to be protective of myself more than ever these days.
This is something else I've been called to do.
Caring for oneself through the grieving process takes effort...
some days more, some days less, depending on many factors.

One has to learn how to put value on 'the self' and on self-care on a daily basis.
And for some (myself included), this doesn't come easy.....but I AM learning.

I was always the giver... always the empath and largely ignored my self.
Now I'm called to give to myself daily...
to empathise with myself daily.
I am called not to play down or negate the struggles I face,
but to use the strength I've developed, to face the storms when they arise.

Grief has taught me a lot about self-love.
And for that, I am truly grateful.

Not everyone is going to understand you.
Not everyone is going to understand your grief.
Not everyone is going to understand the depth and unpredictability
of the pain you feel,
and how it can change from one day to the next.

Not even those closest to you.

Not everyone is going to understand that you can't just move on.
Not everyone is going to understand that your life has changed
and so have you.

Not everyone is going to want you to change.
Not everyone is going to understand
that it's the connection with your loved one that sustains you,
and keeps you going, keeps you moving forward each day.

Not everyone is going to understand
why you work on deepening that connection.
Not everyone is going to understand
that you love and long to talk about them.
Not everyone is going to understand that you can't leave them behind
... even if it were possible.
Not everyone is going to understand
the depth of love you carry in your heart for them.

Not everyone is going to understand........

There were many times I hid how I felt from others.
Many times I put on a brave face, because somehow it felt easier
than explaining how I felt,
knowing that it was almost impossible
for others to understand.
I didn't really understand grief myself just yet.
I was in uncharted waters,
swimming for dear life,
searching for a life raft
to cling onto.

A Good Friend
(can be hard to find)

I can't take away your pain,
but I can sit with you while you cry
and wipe away the tears from your face.
I can't do anything to change
what has happened.
But I can listen to you,
as you tell me the truth about how you feel,
as many times as you need to ,
to ease your pain.
I can't see things through your eyes,
but I can look with you,
as you begin to imagine what life
will be like for you now ... in the future.
I can't turn back the clock,
to who you were before.
But I can promise to love the new version
of you, who is emerging,
from the fiery flames you've entered.
I can't walk this path for you,
but I can offer a hand to steady you,
as you take each tentative step
into the unknown.
I can't make you feel better,
by telling you you'll feel different tomorrow,
or next week, or next month.
But I can be there for you
to weather the storms with you,
in the weeks and months ahead.
I can't change things for you.
I can't take away your pain,
or turn back time.
But I can be a good friend
and sit with you
while you heal.

We are not called to 'move on'
when our loved one leaves for our spiritual home
before us,
just to 'move forward' with our life,
even when sometimes we feel we are
being disloyal.

Yes!
I was surprised by this thought
and the accompanying emotions,
when they arrived unannounced!

Grief assured me that living my life
was in no way being disloyal to my son.
After all, he was right there....
living alongside me.

And my son had always been more carefree than I.
So I may have to learn to be more carefree too...

Keep affirming 'I'll be OK', 'I'll be OK'...
These were words that ran through my mind in the early days.
I had to keep affirming to myself that I would survive the death of my son
and that at some point in the future...I would be OK.
I knew that sending positive thoughts to my mind, was also helping my body to heal,
as both are intrinsically linked. I recall that my body often felt heavy and cumbersome
and there were days when I literally had to drag myself out of bed to meet the day.
But I always managed it somehow.....even if sometimes it was late afternoon.
Something inside me knew the path I needed to follow to begin to heal
and something inside me knew that it was not only possible to survive this trauma,
<u>but to eventually thrive.</u>
So I followed that something....I clung to it like a life-raft,
and allowed it teach me all I needed to know.
I was an eager student, always sitting at the front of the class, listening intently.
Slowly, things began to fall into place, my vision became clearer, my heart began to mend.
I wouldn't ever be the same person as 'before',
I instinctively knew that... and that was OK.
I hoped I would have more understanding, more compassion
and eventually more capacity for joy in my life,
because I no longer worried about things that were insignificant.
And a great deal of things seemed insignificant when placed beside my son's 'death'.
I wasn't afraid to die for one thing, but also,
I was getting to the point where I wasn't afraid to live, either.
If life wasn't finished with me yet, I wanted to see what she had in store.
I wanted to see the role she had in mind for me.
I wanted to discover 'a purpose' in all the pain, one might say.
Life eventually opened my eyes to see, that 'to love', is really the only purpose I need.
It may sound like a cliche, but love was the answer to almost every question I had.
So now, I feel more than OK...most days
And on the days that I don't, I reaffirm that I AM OK, and soon the heaviness passes.
I begin each day with the words...
<u>Today is a good day,</u> and watch it unfold.
I try to stay mostly in the present, this took some practice, but this way,
I provide the day with an opportunity to reveal itself to me and I flow along with it.
Grief tells me.....
"The day is already written, just show up and allow it to support you"
So I just show up, and do what life asks of me....
because at the end of the day, what more can I do?
Life takes care of life.....
This is what I have begun to experience ... and come to trust.

Grief often calls on us to make a huge shift
in our belief system.
Depending on what we have been taught,
or the culture we were brought up in,
this can be a small,
or a colossal change.
Some may decide
not to make the change,
for others,
they can't not.

What we leave behind.

I had nothing much to hang onto when you left.
You didn't care much for things.
You didn't collect objects, the way some of us do.
And clothes you'd say, are just something to cover your skin,
so why get so worked up about them?

So there was very little left of you for me to hang onto,
when you bowed out of life.
Nothing to show to the world that you existed.

And I envied those who had memory bears,
lovingly created from carefully chosen items
their loved ones once wore,
on which their unique scent still lingered.
Or those who had rooms full of memories,
wrapped up in trinkets that their loved ones held dear.

But you my dear child, you travelled lightly through life,
barely kissing the earth with your feet, lest you leave an imprint.

'Oh', I hear you say...
'What about the imprint I left on the hearts of others...
Do they not count?'
And I thought about that for a moment or two
and I had to agree...
that what you left,
wasn't to be found in anything tangible
It was to be found in the way your spirit flows with such surety,
through those who were given the gift of loving you,
for even a brief moment in time.

And that I feel, is more than enough for me to hold onto,
for however much time remains.

A simple thing to do each morning
before getting out of bed.
Place your hands together,
as if in prayer.

Interlock your fingers and
squeeze your palms together.
This is a reminder of just how close
you and your loved ones truly are.

Learning to embrace the Spirit World ... A journey into the unknown.

I come from there...
and there, I shall one day return...
To my true essence.
Even as my mortal body turns to dust
to become a single grain...
a speck in a boundless desert,
blowing in the sands of time.
One day...one day soon,
I will return to the essence
in which you now dwell.
But for now, I am still a child of the earth
and you,
you are a child of stardust
of moonlight ... of sunbeams
blowing in the winds of Utopia.
While I walk the land of mere mortals,
you,
you dance with angels
and have conversations with mystics around the dinner table.
While I wrestle with life's many challenges,
of a worldly order,
you,
you are as free as the elusive bird of paradise,
that glides overhead
and gazes down on where
you once walked this land
and danced, and played and loved.
Oh how I long to taste the freedom
that you encounter
How I long to dance with angels
and talk with mystics,
under the stars, on a moonlit night.
But wait, I hear you say
What's stopping you?
And I realise
I alone set my limitations...
by believing I am merely the mortal self.
And of course, you remind me I'm not.
And I listen, because after all,
you dance with angels and have
conversations with mystics,
So when you say how could I be less than who I truly am...?
I listen...

Grief has shown me
that it's entirely possible
to feel both heartbroken and happy at the same time.
Yes, there may always be that heartbreak present in my life.
It's how grief shows up in my body.
Yet at the same time,
I also have the capacity to feel happy,
hopeful, grateful, joyous and glad to be alive!
I can go from tears to laughter in an instant....
and from laughter to tears too.
The whole range of human emotions are alive within me!

When you died, my world turned upside down
.... or at least that's what it felt like.
Nothing made sense anymore.
I had to question almost everything I knew.
And through the questioning and answers I received,
I came to realise,
that far from being upside down,
my world was being turned right-side up,
so I could see the truth of things.
The truth of birth and death,
of right and wrong,
of good and bad.
All conceptions and misconceptions were on the table in-front of me,
inviting me to take a look at what I thought of as 'truth'.

I was called to question everything I knew or thought I knew.
My so-called stable existence, was rocked to the core.
Everything felt uncertain, in-spite of my thinking that I
was 'aware', spiritually speaking.
What would the future hold ?
This was the next chapter of my life
and life was asking for my input on how it would be written.
I was constantly being invited to look deeper
into life's mysteries.
Near death experiences, after-death communication, out of body experiences.
Phenomenon little explored until now.
Constantly life was calling me to look...to seek...to find.
I knew my son's presence was hidden among these mysteries somewhere,
so I took up the invitation
and discovered so much more than I ever thought I would.

And I'm still exploring...
Still discovering.
And I am truly thankful to life for encouraging me,
out of the darkness and into the light.

No matter how long it has been,
there will be days when you will simply feel fragile,
just as there will be days when you will feel a little stronger.
On these fragile days,
treat yourself with the care of a small seedling,
just beginning to push up through the earth
to catch the nourishing rays of the morning sun.
Feed yourself with
tenderness, love and understanding.
Water the garden of your soul
with affection.
Look for and lean on the support around you.
Just as the gardener may plant a stick
to help the emerging sapling,
we too, need this kind of support
until we are strong enough to stand firmly
on our own once again.
And when we ARE strong enough
and standing firmly....
we can reach out and be a support for others like us,
who are also in the healing place,
in this great garden of life.

Dream Visits

I will meet you in the silence
On that long forgotten trail
High above the mountains
Beneath the thinning of the veil

......

I will meet you in the clearing
Beside the willow tree
Waiting there, is a special place
Reserved for you and me

....

I'll meet you under starlight
When the moon is shining bright
When all but we are sleeping
In the silence of the night.

......

We will talk about tomorrow
And plan the road ahead
I will answer all the questions
That are floating round your head

......

I will comfort, I will soothe you
I'll plant a kiss upon your face
I'll assure you you will be okay
In the warmth of my embrace

......

So come meet me in your dream-time
On that long forgotten trail
You'll find me under our Willow Tree
I'll be waiting there ......without fail

Many people I know, have had dreams or dream visitations from their loved ones.
Some friends I know, have had several.
Me, I'm still patiently waiting , even though I say to my son every night... 'see you in my dreams'.

The way our loved ones come through to us are many and varied.
And I am reminded that I need to embrace the possibility that one night I may just get a dream visit.
Until then, I will be grateful for all of the other signs my son sends me.

Healing, or wanting to heal
after the death of a loved one,
doesn't mean you love them any less,
or miss them any less.
Many people feel guilty for what they see as
'getting on with their lives',
or even having the thought of wanting to.
But we should not feel guilty over something that deep down,
we all want for ourselves.
The desire to feel better...
The desire for joy and happiness in our lives...
These desires are inherent in us all.
Yet for the one who is grieving,
these thoughts,
these natural human desires,
often play tricks on our minds.

Who Understands me, but me?

Grief has shown me things about myself I never would have known.
She has shown me strength
that has lain dormant
waiting,
patiently,
knowing its day would come.

For grief knows the plans of the Creator
and stores up strength
for those who'll need it,
when their time comes.

Grief has shown me there is purpose in the pain.
She has shown me the beauty
in the breaking open of ones' heart
to all of life's hidden mysteries,
never explored
until called to.

For grief knows the plans of the Creator
and stores up purpose
for those who'll need it
when the time comes.

Grief has shown me beauty within the bleakness
She has shown me joy in the simplest of things.
Things I never would have experienced,
never would have been exposed to,
until called to do so.

For grief knows the plans of the Creator
and stores up beauty
for those who'll need it
when the time comes.

Who understands me but me?
Grief tells me <u>she</u> does.

May we all find moments of peace and joy today.
May we smile at the little things.
May we notice what's important.
May we embrace whatever challenges the day brings
with renewed hope in our hearts.
We've come through so much already...to arrive here...
at this moment in time.
May we remember always,
what has brought us this far...

I come to the ocean with enticing regularity.
She draws me to her with her silent call.
Come...
Sit with me a while...
Let me wash away the heaviness you carry.
Let me wash away the doubt, the fear, the insecurity
Let me renew your strength and send you on your way...
Rejuvenated...
Replenished...
Refreshed...
The ocean has been my saviour in times of need
and I wonder how to repay her.
She wants for nothing it seems,
yet something tells me she has a message to share.
And maybe this is how I can repay her.
I can share her message of
weathering the storms,
of watching the seasons come and go.
Of days overflowing with joy and fun and laughter
to be treasured,
then let go.....
as people arrive and depart her shoreline.
I can share her message of peace
when sunlight falls and moonlight
casts its glow on her surface
and she feels the pull of its energy.
And she rises and falls with the gentleness of the waves,
lulling her softly to sleep...
content,
and silent in the knowing
that all is well.

'Pain is inevitable...
Suffering is optional....'
These were words reportedly spoken by the Buddha.
But what do they mean....Especially for one who is grieving?

There is no doubt that 'losing' someone we love is incredibly painful.
The emotions of grief, can rock us to our core,
often bringing us to our knees.
If we remember that all this is 'normal',
we can begin to allow ourselves to experience the fullness
of the inevitable 'pain of grief', as it rises and falls.

On my journey with grief, I have found that over time, the pain does lessen,
and we begin to emerge from the shock and devastation,
to survey our lives from a new perspective.
We realise that no amount of wishing,
pleading or praying that things were different,
can alter the reality we now find ourselves in.

I've often explored these words of the Buddha, in context to my grief,
and I've come to understand more fully,
the wisdom behind these words.

In my exploration, I came to understand that the pain of 'loss'
was inevitable and nothing could change that.
I had 'lost' someone I loved and
sorrow was something I would have to get used to.
But I also knew that the pain of it, would soften over time.

So if pain is inevitable, how is suffering optional?

More exploration, helped me to understand,
that my thoughts are capable of making me suffer,
beyond the normal pain of grief.
If I dwelt too long in painful and negative thoughts like...
How could this have happened?
This shouldn't be allowed to happen.
Life's unfair.
Why do bad things happen to good people?
God is punishing me, etc.

cont...

cont...

If I kept revisiting these thoughts time and time again, just focusing on the negative,
I felt in my heart (and my body) that I was adding to my pain,
and therefore, adding to my suffering.

The flip side of this is, I realised that I was also equally capable of bringing myself some relief
from my suffering, by changing the direction of my thoughts.
As soon as I realised, they were leading me in a downward spiral,
I could move away from them in different ways....
I could focus on a more positive thought, or happy memory.
I could try to feel the love of my child, ask him for some help and guidance etc.
As I write about this here, I know that it is by no means easy,
especially in the early weeks and months, when grief all but consumes us,
but it is something I found worth exploring and persisting with as I went further into my journey.

I realised that every time I argued with reality, I'd lose.

So I adopted 3 principles and I still stick by them today.
They help me to live alongside grief.
They help me keep things in perspective.
They help me to heal.

1) I do not have the power to change my reality regarding my son's 'death'.
2) If I argue with 'what is', I suffer more.
3) If I accept 'what is', (even if I don't want to),
I release myself perhaps, from additional suffering.

Yes, the pain of losing someone I love is still present,
it always will be.
But I choose not to add to that pain by arguing with reality.

Truth is, we will all feel the pain of grief, when someone we love returns to spirit.
This is the nature of 'being human'.
We miss their physical presence, even if we know they truly are... 'still present'.

But we can reduce our suffering by remembering that grieving is perfectly normal
and that it _is_ possible to survive (and thrive), after a devastating loss.

The wisdom behind the words...
Pain is inevitable...Suffering is optional,
can be a good starting point on our healing journey.

Dan loved being outdoors when he was young.
This photograph was taken half way up
Mount Snowdon, the highest mountain in Wales, UK.
Dan was 10 years old at the time and took the long climb, all in his stride.

This is something I often do to relax, and relieve the stress
that can so often accompany the grieving process....

Find a quiet spot where you won't be disturbed.
Close your eyes and relax.
Take a few deep breaths in and out
(counting the breaths may help)
Now visualise, or imagine yourself wrapped in a
beautiful white blanket of light,
being sent from your loved ones in spirit.
Feel it permeating your body, releasing
any tension from your shoulders, your back,
and anywhere that feels heavy.
Keep your mind focused on the light,
as it washes through your body.
See if you can feel any sensations that come up.

This is how I began to feel my son's presence,
like tingles down one side of my face and body.

The ability of our loved ones in spirit,
to send us signs of their devotion and love
never ceases to amaze me

The outline on the glass, appeared as if by magic.
Through the steam it made its presence known.
Unseen before that moment.
Had I drawn it myself with an invisible hand?
Two interconnecting lines...
curved together as if caressing one another
into a crowning symbol of love...
of our love
of the love we share
on a surface open to to receiving it.
The glinting beam of the morning sun,
nodded its approval.
An imperfectly, perfect heart.
A visual reminder of a love
you are calling me to recognise...
now,
as I stand here alone,
silently praying to the warm water
cascading over my broken body,
to cleanse not only my skin
but the deepest parts of my soul.
Imploring it to wash away the regrets
the failures, the would haves, could haves, should haves,
into the twisting u-bends of the plumbing,
to mix with the debris
of times long forgotten
or those I wish not to recall,
or re-live.
The heart...
an outline, appearing on the glass.
A heart...
Two curved lines that intertwine.
Two curved lines that say... I love you
I care
I'm here
I understand
You are not alone
A heart...
Drawn from your very breath.
Drawn from the vapour of your love.
Drawn onto the smooth surface of the glass.
Drawn onto the broken surface of my heart.

Sometimes, we need to pause,
and look back at how far we've come,
to appreciate just how much healing
is taking place

♡

At some point on this journey, I began questioning exactly when it was that I realised,
I could not only live in this crazy world without your physical presence,
but begin to enjoy all of its magic and mystery...
All of its opportunities for growth....All of its ups and downs.
And then I realised, this is what I've been doing right from the very start....
Right from the very moment that I got the phone-call to say you'd gone....
From that very moment I began to realise that I could live through this....
grow from this....and maybe become a better person...
a more understanding and compassionate person.
Yes....from that very first moment, it began to happen.
Not consciously at first, of course.
To begin with, I wondered how I would ever be able to take the next breath !
But of course, I did....Life breathed life into me, during those first dark days and weeks.
Life carried me along gently, lovingly....on a wave of compassion.
Life literally took care of me, because at that moment,
She (Life), knew I wasn't able to take care of myself.....
Life put me to sleep at night and life woke me up in the morning.
She brought the people I needed around me,
She helped me to dress in the morning and didn't mind if I chose not to some days.
Life literally took care of me!
Then She began to whisper in my ear.....
She began to help me remember things I'd long forgotten.
She began to remind me of where I'd come from and why I was here.
She began to challenge me to 'wake up' to myself....to wake up from the dream that I was in.
She began to encourage me to remember the promises that were made a long time ago.
Promises that I would always be OK, no matter what happens.
That this 'tragedy', was not some form of punishment, or some random act,
but something that had the potential to help me to grow....
something that could help lift the veil between this world and the next...
something that could connect the both.... and from that,
things would emerge that would never have been possible.
And most importantly, She let me know that you weren't 'gone'...
That you were still 'here' .... That you were a part of this journey....Our journey...
A journey into the 'unknown'. Yet what was first 'unknown ',
has begun to feel familiar.....
You are my rock...My safe place...My 'go to' person.
Granted you're not as wild as you sometimes were on earth, but now I get to experience the 'whole' of
your being.... the wisdom, the compassion, the gentleness, the understanding....
Your true nature....Your soul.
And you encourage me to remember that this is who I am, too.
And this is how we connect .... Soul to beautiful Soul.

Often,
I have found,
if I'm patient,
if I wait,
if I trust,
Grief will reveal to me
all I need to know

If I told you that I sometimes feel grateful for having my son in Spirit,
would you think it wrong of me to say that?
Would you think, how can a mother say such a thing?
Does she not want him alive, living a happy life ?

If I were to explain the meaning behind these words, maybe you would understand.
Firstly, my son is such a guiding light in my life, a confidant, a trustworthy friend.
An unconditional love flows between us, that has helped sustain me,
through all of my struggles with grief and I am so grateful to him for that.

Secondly, my son endured many difficulties in life before he died...
He endured many an inner (and outer) battle with mental health and addiction.
A battle that was hard on him, and sheer agony for a mother to bear witness to.

Having a loved one in pain, for whatever reason, and being powerless to 'fix it',
feels like a knife to the heart, yet some of us are called to endure this pain,
and if we are fortunate, it doesn't completely destroy us.
When my son left his body, I knew it was a release for him.
And I know that he knew, it was a release for me, too.

Our lives were, and still are, so interconnected with lessons and shared experiences.
It took me a while to understand the complexity (and the beautiful simplicity) of it all.
But in seeking to understand,
I discovered the deeper truth behind the 'time-span' of a human life...
The entry and exit into this 'world' and the impact on others, a person's life has......
And the Divine plan of it all.
The connection my son and I shared in life, wasn't severed by 'death'....
It was strengthened.

If we are open to accepting that life is eternal, we will understand
that the lessons and teachings that bound us together in this lifetime, continue.
And these teachings from our loved ones in the light, can beautifully enrich our Souls
and expand us beyond anything we could have imagined,
had they not left when they did.

So when I say I am eternally grateful for having my son in spirit, perhaps you will understand that it is
because I know I can never be parted from him.
Would I want him back, living a happy life? Of course I would.
But that option was never open to me.
So I have to make sense of, and learn to fully embrace, where life is leading us both.

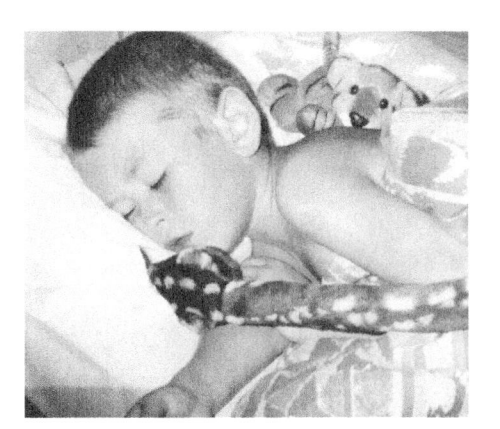

TAKE   PHOTOS

Take photos!
Take hundreds of photos!
Thousands even...
Take photos of special days and those ordinary days too.
Take photos of crazy nights out and cosy nights in-front of the fire,
when a warm blanket is all you need for comfort.
Take photos of birthdays, Christmas, anniversaries,
Take photos at weddings
and at life-celebrations too.
Take photos of newborns, of toddlers,
of teenagers
(even though they may protest).
Take photos of parents, of grandparents, cousins, siblings and friends.
Take photos on exotic holidays
and lazy days in the garden on a Sunday afternoon,
when family or friends drop by, unexpectedly.
Take photos of daring adventures that leave you breathless,
and those quiet times,
when togetherness is all that really matters.
Take photos of those with big beaming smiles who are posing for the camera
... and those who aren't looking, so that you capture their essence,
that inner beauty that's rarely seen.
Take photos of those who are easy to love
and those who challenge you to love them unconditionally.
Take photos when you meet
and photos when you part.
Take photos.
Take plenty of photos.
Make memories...every opportunity you get.
One day, you may search for those memories, like you are mining for gold.
You will search for them, like you are searching for priceless treasure.
And when you find one, you will gaze upon it like an exquisite piece of art.
And you will trace the contours of their face with your fingers
and remember the softness of their skin and how their eyes gazed back at you.
You will recall the time that you took that photo
and you will be so glad that you did.

Take photos...
Make memories...
Memories to last you a lifetime.

It's not uncommon to want to shut oneself off from the outside world
when one is grieving.
I know I did, especially in the early days.
I didn't want to meet anyone I knew and have them ask awkward questions.
Questions like 'How are you doing?'
Or if they hadn't heard the news..."How is your son doing?"
Or a chance meeting with a stranger
and having to answer that question that often crops up in conversation....
'How many children do you have?'

In the early months of grief, normal conversation, seems far from normal.
Your emotions are so close to the surface,
and you are wary of breaking down in front of someone,
so there is a tendency to isolate oneself.
This may be okay for a while, but there comes a time
when you have to rejoin the world.

Take your own time with this, grief told me.
'There's no rush'.
'Try going out somewhere quiet', she said one day when I needed encouraging.
'Somewhere there are less people about'.

So I walked a lot on my own....
in the countryside and by the ocean.
I appreciated the fresh air and the sunshine and I talked to my son,
....in my mind and out loud.
I knew he was right there with me, supporting me in my efforts.
He did a lot to help me in those early weeks and months (and still does).
And I didn't have to tell anyone about our walks.
It was our special time together.

Later, these 'walks' became mini adventures, as life began to open up for me again.
But to begin with, they were walks that soothed my Soul ...
and kept me from falling apart.

Sometimes my son will pop words into my mind and I know I have to quickly write them down.
This poem was 'dictated' by him, early one morning, as I was lying in bed.
I feel it's a message to all of us, who have loved ones in spirit.

Take a gentle walk with me

When your heart feels heavy
And your mind has lost control
Take a gentle walk with me
To soothe and heal your Soul
We can talk about how you miss me
We can just walk hand in hand
We can gaze upon the vista
I can make you understand
I haven't ever left your side
I'm with you every day
You need not ever say goodbye
I never went away
My body held no use for me
My spirit longed to soar
I know it's hard to understand
When 'death' knocks on your door
The choice I made was easy
There was no holding back
When your time comes you'll understand
There's nothing that I lack
I don't miss out
I don't regret
I always walk in faith
My biggest triumphs
My smallest deeds
They all fell into place
Life on earth is tricky
When you have a 'human' mind
Things get muddled up sometimes
And peace is hard to find
So when your heart feels heavy
And your mind has lost control
I invite you to take a walk with me
So I can soothe your soul

Triggers and healing

There are many things that trigger us, when we are grieving.
I was reminded of this one Sunday morning, when I tuned into a local radio station,
just as a particularly poignant song was playing.
The strength of emotions that shot through my body,
took me completely by surprise
and I just cried....and cried...and cried.

I was completely present, but unable to stop the tears from flooding out,
or the emotions that rocked my body to the core.
In my mind, I knew enough to let them just happen, but I also knew
that I still disliked intensely, this feeling of utter despair.
These triggers, can take us right back to the early days of grief....
and I don't like to revisit that time.

I was conscious enough to watch my accompanying thoughts,
to make sure they didn't get out of control.
I knew where my thoughts wanted to take me,
and I knew well enough, that it doesn't serve me to go there,
so I was able to pull myself back from the brink
and just let the emotions run their course.

Grief is complicated! .... is what I've come to understand these past few years.
I'm still learning and I'm sure I shall continue learning
for the foreseeable future.

What was interesting, was something I came across the next day,
as I was sitting in my favourite coffee shop.
I was reading a book I had been drawn to a few weeks earlier.
I always take note of books I'm drawn to,
as I've learnt that they almost always contain something of value to me.
The chapter I was reading, informed me,
that we do not have to revisit the past
to _heal_ the past.
We have the ability to heal the past,
in the present moment....

cont.....

cont...

So my emotional outpouring took on a whole new meaning for me.
Yes, I certainly know there are things that are locked away inside of me,
that I don't want to, or are not ready to look at.
Past experiences....things I wish I'd done differently,
had I known the outcome.

But I also know that by revisiting, or reliving the past over and over in my mind,
only serves to reinforce those emotions,
and NOT help them to heal.

The body, mind and soul are a marvellous combination.
When I stop and think about it, I am in awe of how they work together.
And I choose to believe that mine are always working toward healing.
I believe this to be true for us all.

So I viewed it as part of life's amazing synchronicity and connectivity,
that following my emotional outpouring on Sunday,
I was led to this valuable information the very next day ....
and THAT to me is miraculous.
The realisation that we CAN heal the past in the present
is a game changer for me.

I understand now, that the tears and the accompanying pain when it comes,
are both serving to heal my past trauma
and in so doing,
are healing my broken heart.

So now I am able to much more readily accept these emotions when they arise.
Of course I have to stay present....
to not let the thoughts run wild,
and reinforce the experiences that caused them in the first place.
But by doing so,
I can be comforted by the fact that my wise and wonderful being,
is healing me, gently ... bit by bit,
and I can fully embrace all that I am
and all that I am becoming, as it does so.

Grief has taught me this....

Oh Grief...
You create in me a roller coaster of emotions.
One day up,
the next day down.
Unpredictable as you are...
the unknown lurking around every corner.
Occasionally,
you offer me an exhilarating ride,
when you show me glimpses of things
previously unseen.
That invisible thread of connection we share
with those who are free.
Free from the encumbrance of a body I still cling to.
Other days,
I am thrown headlong into your
deep, frightening nose-dives,
where I wonder if I will stay in my seat,
or be cast adrift, with little or no support.
All too often,
I've been thrown into the abyss
of loss and misery,
as the ride you take me on,
dips and swerves.
And I hang on while you whisper to me...
'Trust'

<u>Grief.</u>
<u>A roller-coaster ride.</u>

I never liked these particular rides at the fairground.
And if I'm perfectly honest with Grief,
I'm not entirely sold on this ride she's taking me on, either....

How are you doing?
A question we hear many times along this journey...
And our answer is often...I'm doing OK.
Not necessarily because we ARE doing OK,
but to try to explain ourselves, often seems too complicated.
So I began after a while, to ask this question of myself...
How am I doing? How am I really doing?
Looking back, I realise from the very beginning,
I was determined that this heartbreaking 'loss', would not destroy me.
I wasn't sure at the time if I could pull it off,
but I was sure that the strength that was inside of me,
my very beautiful soul would rise up and carry me forward.
And thankfully she did.
And she continues to do so.
I honour her for the wonderful way she has shown me that we don't 'die.'
Dying is impossible, she says....We are all eternal beings.
We come from spirit, and we return to spirit.
This life is but a brief interlude.
I was blessed to have 'seen' my son's spirit form,
in all its glory, a few months into my journey.
He appeared at the end of my bed for the briefest of moments while I was relaxing.
The light that emanated from him was so beautiful,
and a deep sense of peace and love filled my very being.
I began to think of him in that form, instead of his physical form,
and that certainly seemed to help.
I realised in that moment, that before he entered his physical body ....
the body that I knew and loved, he had been this amazing Spirit being.
And after 26 years he dropped the physical body he had borrowed for a while,
returning to his true form, (which grief tells me is, what we will all do one day).

I still miss his physical presence deeply...
his laugh, his smile,
his way of being 'easy' in the world, like nothing really mattered.
But I remind myself of the inner beauty that shines through him,
offering me a guiding light on my path.
Coming to this understanding, took time,
but when we come to realise and fully embrace the truth of our existence,
it can help us to live the rest of our life, in a more peaceful way.

And I oh so want to live life more peacefully.....

One day, during my morning inspired writing practice,
I was feeling a bit low. I know my son always senses this in me
and his words that morning, confirmed this.
He tells me those in spirit, are deeply connected to us, and are
aware when we feel sad, and they are also aware when we feel happy.
They love to see us smile, but they understand our sorrow, too.

"I know that you are grieving
I see it in your eyes
The way you try to hide it
is simply no disguise
I see the very heart of you
I hear your every thought
Just know I come to hold your hand
whenever you're distraught.
Let my tender love enfold you,
and with your heart I'll blend
Surrender to this moment
And allow yourself to mend."

It's LOVE that brings us together...wherever we are

It's love that brings us together
Perhaps we've forgotten along life's way
Return to the love you shared, and find
your loved ones never 'went away'.

This lifetime is one of many
Our spirits have come to play
We'll go through many experiences
forgetting who we are along the way.

But 'death' brings us back together
It holds up a torch so we see
In truth we are are all just playing a part
There's no difference between you and me

If we remember this truth and remember it well
In time we will understand
Our loved ones who've stepped out of life's game
Are now holding us by the hand

They want us to wake up and remember
To open our eyes and see
That nothing on earth can part us
We are closer now, now that they're free

Free from the bodies that house us
Like a trapped bird trained not to fly
Free from that big misunderstanding
'You only live once' is a lie!

In truth our lives are eternal
If we open our hearts to realise
There's so much more to be discovered
Than can be seen with our two human eyes.

It's up to each of us to try to remember
To choose now, and go within
Make that choice to open up your heart
And let the truth come flooding back in.

Not all of us who are grieving are in the same boat.
Some of us have lost a child, a parent, a partner a sibling, a good friend.
Some have suffered a miscarriage, or endured a still-birth.
Some of us have endured a combination of these 'losses'.

We may not all be in the same boat,
but we are all on the same ocean of grief,
facing the storms that come our way.

Some of us feel we only have a life raft,
barely keeping us afloat.
Some of us feel we are drowning, with no form of rescue in sight.
Some of us feel we are frantically paddling a canoe....upstream.
Some, at this moment in time,
may have the relative safety of a more substantial vessel
to assist us on our journey.

Most of us will have a combination of all of the above at some point,
as we navigate these choppy waters of grief.

<u>An invitation from our loved ones ...</u>

Please look for me in the present
You won't find me in the past
There may be some wonderful memories there
But memories... they don't last

I'm here in every moment
I'm in every breath you take
I'm constantly watching over you
I watch every decision you make

I see you sometimes struggling
to be strong and a comfort to all
So I'm here to gently remind you
You can't always shoulder it all

Let me be the light for you
For I see the road ahead
It's paved with many new memories
So come with me there, instead

We can look to a brighter future
One that's exciting and new
Don't worry, you don't have to go it alone
I'll be standing right next to you.

It's an invitation I'm offering
To help you out of this sorrow and pain
Open your heart to new adventures
I promise you, life can be joyous again

Exploring a new way of communication
Let's experience the joy that it brings
I'll open your mind to the unexplored realms
I promise... you won't regret a thing

You have me as your very own 'angel'
Your guiding star... a guiding light
So take a step out of the darkness,
Let me show you a future that's bright.

The promise of a new day

I have a large canvas on the wall in my lounge.
I designed it many years ago.
It has the words

Today is a brand new day!

and a beautiful scene of the sun rising.

I like to be reminded that every day brings with it,
a promise of new possibilities on the horizon.

Every day has potential.
Potential to bring peace and joy into my life.
Whatever yesterday brought,
today is always a brand new day.

When we are grieving, it is helpful
to stay in the present as much as possible.
Here, in the present moment, our loved ones
are accessible to us.
They dwell in the present moment with us.
This is what I've come to believe... and know
and hold onto.

They don't live in the past.
The past are our memories
And even if they are good memories,
they must be brought alive in the present moment,
for us to experience them.

Our loved ones are always with us.
They share in each new dawn,
each new day.

This thought alone, brings me peace.

Music can evoke such strong emotions in one who is grieving.

For the first couple of years, I couldn't listen to any music with lyrics.
I could listen to classical music, which I came to love,
but nothing with lyrics, as it would make me break down in tears.
Slowly, this inability passed, but even now,
music and lyrics combined,
can evoke strong emotions within me.

A friend sent me a song recently,
and on listening to it, the floodgates opened.
I didn't attempt to close them.
I embraced the feeling and realised that these tears that were being shed,
were coming from a place deep within me,
and not attached to anything in particular.
Just sheer emotion,
looking for and finding an opportunity for release.

As I allowed myself to fall into and be held by this act of sorrow,
I felt my son's presence beside me,
his hand on mine,
as I placed it instinctively over my heart.

"I know you understand more than anyone,
how grief can reach such hidden depths,
and pull emotions long buried, to the surface,
to be held to the light", I said quietly.

It may have only been a small amount that was brought to the surface that day,
but I am always, always grateful,
for the wisdom and the grace that surrounds me,
in every desperate moment....
without judgement.

And I am always grateful for my son's comforting presence
throughout every storm.

I feel you moving closer.
Curious, it seems.
And it reminds me of days past,
when you were young,
and things often sparked a curiosity in you.
You explored your world with an eagerness,
lest time should slip away
like the sands of an hourglass...
And now, living in 'no time'
you are equally as curious,
as am I...
to see where this journey will lead us.

Today...

I begin to step forward onto a new path,
a new journey with you.
I don't know where it will lead
but I put my faith and trust in you,
to show me the way.

I want to make new memories with you.
And you told me we would.

I want to travel new paths with you and
meet you where you are now...
and you told me I could.

I want to embrace my grief and
wrap it up in all the love I have for you
and you told me I should.

"All of this takes time" you said.
"But it will be worth the investment".

"There are still so many roads left untraveled.
So many adventures to be had" you said.

"It will take until the end of your lifetime.
And then...
A new adventure will begin".... you said.

I don't want your death to define you
I want your life to be your legacy!
I want your kindness, your compassion
your sheer exuberance for life,
to be what defines you.
But why define me at all ? I hear you say....
Let me be an enigma...
Let me be a part all that you see,
all that you feel, all that you do.
Let me be the light that shines in your eyes,
the tears that fall in sparkles on your cheeks when you think of me.
Let me be the kindness that moves
through your words as you speak ... and as you write.
Let me be the hand that guides your brush as you paint
and let me mingle with the colours
that birth a unique creation into being,
so that when you look at it, all you see is a beauty that reminds you of me.
Let me be free to surprise and delight you
in ways you never expected,
never imagined,
never dreamed of.
Let me be what stops you in your tracks
when you're hurrying much too quickly through life
and missing all that's being laid
like a smorgasbord before you,
for you to merge with and delight in.
Let me be your guiding light,
your north-star,
your wing-man,
your tour guide through life.
Let me open the container of your world
so you can see star light
in the air around you like fire flies,
that invite you to dance with me, in their glow.
Seek not to define me.
Let me be free.
As free as you know, I've always been....
And in doing this, you can be free too...

Grief gatecrashed a perfectly good day today.
So unpredictable is she.
She seldom gives any warning of her arrival.
It was late August, and I was enjoying time in the sun with my daughter and her family.

At a beach-side cafe, a singer was entertaining the crowds.
No sooner had we sat down, when I heard the familiar bars of a song,
that threw me unceremoniously back in time.
Back to a day in April.....April 30th 2019, to be exact.
The day I was told of your 'death'.
Triggers....
There are so many of them in the world of the grieving.
Like un-exploded bombs, waiting to go off.
Just a few bars of the song and my whole body instantly contracted.
Tears sprung to my eyes as I reached for my sunglasses to hide them.
My daughter... she knew without asking.
She glanced my way and whispered...'You OK?'.
I nodded.
To passes by, I may have appeared to be sat at a table, enjoying the afternoon sun,
but in my mind, I was back at a service station cafe,
where a young lad behind the counter, was asking me if I was having a nice evening,
and I was whispering "not really",
while desperately trying to stop the tears from overflowing down my cheeks.
I wanted to add, I've just been told 'my son is dead',
but I knew that would have caused him to feel uncomfortable,
and he didn't deserve that.
He was young.....younger perhaps than my son...
It might have been his first day in the job,
and anyways, at that time, I couldn't bring myself to say those words....
'My son is dead.'
I couldn't bring myself to say those words for the longest of time.
They seemed so final...
So I didn't say them....not that day....
But I noticed through the shock of it all,
that there was a song playing over the speaker system,
and as I listened to the words of that song,
I felt my son was telling me that he was sorry.

The young man, offered me a free coffee... and said he was sorry too.
He didn't know what he was sorry for, but he said it all the same.
And I managed to smile at this small token of kindness,
in a world that was crashing down around me.

There is a little known secret
You may have discovered it recently
It's about our departed loved ones
Those who are special to you and to me.

Not many talk about it
Some may say that we are all mad
Others will shake their heads and sigh
And whisper... 'it's because they are sad'.

But we are not either mad or sad
We're not going 'round the bend'
We have discovered the hidden truth
That death is simply 'not the end'.

Most think we are 'this body'
Just flesh and blood and bone
That this mortal form that we took on
That this is our 'true home'.

But truth is we are spirit
We're light & joy & love
We come from a place that can't be seen
some call it 'Heaven above'.

It's a truth that changes everything
A truth we are seldom shown
That our loved ones are not 'dead and gone'
They've simply gone... 'back home'.

And home is not that far away
There's no distance that we share
If you reach out with your hand you'll find
They really are 'just there!'

You may sense them right beside you
If you close your eyes you'll know
There is no separation
And it's love that makes it so.

Over the years, I have received some incredible signs from my son in spirit.
At first I was a bit sceptical, (even though he was communicating with me
from the moment I received the news of his passing).
I feel it's quite normal and healthy to be a bit sceptical, or discerning,
but if left unquestioned, doubt can become a big barrier,
and can hold us back from fully embracing the possibilities that exist,
for communication between the earthly and spiritual realms.
There are huge amounts of credible pieces of evidence of the existence of the 'afterlife',
so the only thing asked of us, is that we become open to the possibilities.
I was eager and determined from the start, to have the best possible relationship with my son.
Communication hadn't always been easy for us in the later years of his life
and now, I knew that for him at least, those earthly struggles and barriers had been lifted.
I knew that it was just me ... who could potentially hold us back.
He did make it easy for me in the beginning though.
He bombarded me with signs...and the family too.
Feathers, music, special numbers, birds...
His name on billboards, in books, on car number plates...
Electrical items malfunctioning (though I didn't care much for those signs!)

Some of my favourite signs of his presence,
are when he makes people say something, and they have no idea why they said it!
On one occasion, my daughter asked the waiter in a restaurant for banoffee pie,
even though she had just told me she was ordering profiteroles for dessert.
When the waiter placed it in front of her, she whispered to me that she didn't like banofee pie
and had no idea why she asked for it!
We laughed when I told her Dan had mentioned to me once, that it was his favourite dessert!
She still doesn't like it, but we try to eat it every year on his birthday.

On my own birthday, the year after he left, I had a little robin hop onto my knee
and eat out of my hand. It stayed with me for over half an hour, completely unafraid.
I knew it was a birthday gift from Dan.

Most of all, he connects with me through my thoughts and through my writing.
I kept a grief journal from the start and so many times he came through to me this way.

I have seen him in spirit form, beside my bed.
I have felt the bedclothes pulled back at night and felt his warm embrace.
There are countless ways our loved ones can communicate with us.
Trying out different forms of communicating, is like learning a new language...
but far more rewarding.

On this difficult journey,
Grief is always reminding me,
to keep my focus,
to keep hold of my dreams.
And when pain and sorrow arise she says, 'stay with it'...

I have found all of her 'suggestions' extremely helpful
on my journey towards healing my broken heart.
To sit with deep pain and sorrow,
is by no means easy,
but by giving it space,
I have found it begins to transform of its own accord.

Sometimes, Grief encourages me to envisage
a white light entering my body through the top of my head,
and travelling where it needs to go,
to heal that broken part of me.
This simple practice,
can be extremely powerful.

Grief has shown me,
that it helps to be an 'active participant' in my healing journey.

Even in sorrow, we can keep our dreams alive.
We can focus on how we would like our life to be, going forward.
We can allow space for grieving,
and at the same time,
honour those we love ....
as well as our dear selves.

<u>More words from spirit</u>

I'd love for you to feel proud of your self,
Just like I'm so proud of you
I watch you doing the best that you can
I'm in awe of the things that you do

Living without me isn't easy I know
I feel the depth of your pain
I know what your one wish, if granted would be
To have me back by your side once again

If only your eyes could see me
(I've heard that you wish for this, too)
You'd see that I'm always right there by your side
I watch over every small thing that you do.

Not a moment goes by unnoticed
Not a breath that you breathe I don't feel
There's nothing on earth, that ever can break
That contract of love we both sealed

Until your life there is over,
Until all your work there is done,
I will walk by your side,
my heart filled with pride
Because our two hearts now beat as one.

Limited thinking,
acts like a closed door
between the mundane and the miraculous.
Opening that door,
and letting go of beliefs that no longer serve us,
and embracing new possibilities,
is an invitation open to us all.
Accepting and acting upon that invitation,
is our true work.

New Possibilities

AWAIT

Acceptance...
Not easy,
but I found,
it became necessary on the road to healing.
Some have asked me how I can possibly
accept the death of my son
and I answer...I didn't have a choice.
To not accept the facts, would have
led to more suffering and
I knew I couldn't bear that.
Acceptance doesn't mean
I like what happened, I tell them.
It simply means
that I can't change what has happened,
no matter how much
I wish and pray things were different.
Non-acceptance, I tell them,
would be me, arguing with reality
and no-one has ever
won that particular war.
And I didn't want a war.
I didn't want a battle to add to the torment
I was already feeling.
I knew that whatever I did
I couldn't change things..
I couldn't bring my son back.
I simply don't have that power.

I found accepting, <u>enabled me</u>.
It enabled me to discover ways to begin to heal,
so I was no longer a helpless bystander,
tossed about by life.

Acceptance asks just one thing of us...
to allow it to provide a doorway to help us heal....

Healing

On writing the previous page, about ACCEPTANCE,
and knowing how hard a concept it is for a lot of people,
because of the various connotations of the word itself,
my son asks me to write about how acceptance has helped me
in other ways too.

He reminds me that I've learned to accept all of the following :

I've learned to accept that he still lives on, just in a new form.
That death is certainly not the end of life.
That he is available to me in his 'new form' whenever I call on him.
That there are many realities (or dimensions), not just the earth plane.
That life is eternal and I <u>will</u> get to see him again and that he will be the first in line to greet me,
when my time comes to leave my body behind.

I've also learned to accept:

That life can bring happiness to live alongside loss,
and it's perfectly OK to feel a joy for living again.
I have accepted that I have the strength to see this lifetime through
and that my son works alongside me, to make sure of it.
I've learned to accept that there is beauty and purpose to every lifetime, whatever its length.
I've learned to accept that I'm never alone on this journey.
That there is so much more 'truth' yet to be discovered.
That my son has the map and is leading the way for me to follow.

All of the above, I have learned to accept and as my journey continues,
I know there will be much more to learn ...and accept into my life.

Life with our loved ones across the veil, can be a difficult and challenging journey,
but there exists within it the possibility that it can also be a beautiful and enlightening journey, too....
I have chosen to <u>embrace this possibility</u>!

And I have to tell you, it has made
ALL THE DIFFERENCE!

I sometimes hear from people who are concerned that their loved ones passed alone.
There was a time when I felt this way too.
My son died in a place belonging to someone he knew.
In the early days, I know I caused myself to suffer,
by imagining he was all alone when he died, and the thought broke my heart.
But after some research, I realised that these were just thoughts
and they had no basis in actual truth.
Yes, on the outside, it may have appeared that my son was alone when he passed to spirit, but in truth,
I discovered after much researching and conversation, we are never alone....ever.
I discovered that we come into this world as a part of a unique team, (whether we realise it or not).
We are after all... spirits having a human experience.
Our spirit team is extremely dedicated to us. They look upon us as the 'figure head' so to speak.
We are at the cutting edge of this human experience and they are riding along beside us,
every step of the way. Our experience is their experience too.
They provide guidance and advice when we ask for it and offer us support too.
They are not there to intervene in our decisions,
but they do support us, in whatever choices we make in life.
My son was very aware of the spirit side of life from a young age,
though I know he largely ignored it,
and rarely spoke about it to anyone but me, as he grew older.
In addition to the out of body experiences he had as a child,
he visually saw what I believe were his spirit team.
4 or 5 of them he said, in his room one night, a few years before he passed.

When my Mum was ill, she spoke of her loved ones in spirit, being with her
as she lay in her hospital bed, as if it were the most natural thing in the world......
because of course, it is.

For anyone who feels concerned that their loved one passed alone,
please know that they were never alone.
Their team would be there with them whatever the circumstances
and their soul family too, waiting to welcome them home.
Grief is a difficult enough road as it is,
so questioning some of the thoughts that make us suffer,
lifts the burden just a bit and allows us to let more light into our lives.
Our loved ones ARE the light...... and now,
in addition to our spirit team, we have someone very special watching over us.

Knowing this, makes me feel truly blessed.

I have a collection of feathers
and all the other wonderful signs you've sent me.
They are a treasure trove of your love...

It's OK, NOT be OK sometimes,
is what Grief tells me in our conversations.
She tells me it's not always possible, or indeed healthy,
to negate feelings of deep sadness and despair when they arise.
She's taught me enough about these emotions to know that they all pass....sooner or later.
So when something triggered me into an uncontrollable outburst of tears recently,
I just went with it....No questions asked.

Riding the storm has become familiar.
It certainly isn't comfortable ... and often deeply painful,
and this particular storm was fierce, but I recognised its purpose
and the challenging thoughts it brought up.

What triggered it, was that I'd come across something my son had written,
a year or so before he passed, about how addiction often made him feel lonely,
isolated...misunderstood...and worse of all, judged by others,
and by society as a whole... who he said, continually fail to understand this illness.
He wrote that he often pushed away those he loved
and he was attempting to explain why.
On reading his words, strong and uncomfortable emotions,
that his struggle with addiction had caused in me over many long years,
came flooding to the surface as fast as the tears could fall from my eyes...
Grief engulfed me and swept me along on a tidal wave and I hung on for dear life,
knowing (thankfully) that at some point it would run out of energy
and throw me onto the sandbanks, to recover and lick my wounds.

The beauty of it was, I felt my son's presence during this storm.
He stood by the side of me, not attempting to rescue me,
just a strong, comforting presence...
.... a lighthouse, is how he described himself later,
to make sure I was safe in the storm.

He tells me that throughout his struggles, this is how he saw me....
His lighthouse in the storm.
He tells me I was never meant to save him, it was enough to know I was there,
a beacon of strength, a guiding light.
And now the roles are reversed, he says...
And now I understand.
And my mind returns to a state of peace and grace, once again....
Our loved ones are always aware of our struggles
and offer us what they can by means of support.

They know their very presence, can be of great comfort to us.

Forming a picture in my mind
of how my son appears now,
in the fullness of his being,
free of the earthly costume he once wore,
helps me to feel
closer to him, somehow.

Oh to see you again in your magnificence
like I've seen you many times before.
Now.
As I stand here in the absence of your being,
I remember those sunny days
when we watched birds drift on the wing,
and caught butterflies in the meadow.
Those times of freedom felt jubilant...
like they would last forever,
yet alas,
nothing does.
Everything transforms,
even you my dear one,
even you.
And I can glimpse you now,
in your magnificent splendour.
I can see you now....
As you really are...
As you've always been...
As you always were...
Together, we will be.... once again.
When springtime turns to summer,
autumn to winter
....we shall remain.
Transformed yes,
but still here to touch the earth and the sky
and to rest,
like the birds on the wing,
floating gracefully,
in our true splendour.

The words on the opposite page,
were 'dictated' by my son one morning,
when I asked him the question,
'What was it like, to die'?
When I read it back,
my heart filled with immense joy.
This journey of writing with him
is certainly a most joyous experience.

What is it, to die? I ask
To die, you say,
is to feel the blessed release
of a soul that knows it is homeward bound.

To die you say,
is to know that you have lived this life fully,
for the purpose it was intended....
....this time around.

To die, you say
is to soar with the force of a majestic geyser,
rising up from the ground into the welcoming arms of the sky
to merge with the stars unseen,
yet felt with such a rush of exuberance it moves the very breath out of you,
that needs to be left behind.

To die, you say,
is to see colours impervious to the human eye,
flashing past you in a kaleidoscope of patterns
that merge with your very being,
enfolding you in a time-capsule of memory, an instant reminder,
that where you are headed....
although temporarily forgotten, is remembered instantly,
and feels so familiar now.

To die you say
is to feel the warmth and love of
a thousand 'strangers'
who have come to your side
to welcome you home from a voyage,
that they're aware
you carry a suitcase full of wisdom from,
that you will unlock and share with them later,
around the campfire,
on the open prairie
that has already been prepared in your honour.

To die you say,
is to fully dissolve into yourself....
and know that you are home,
among friends,
once again.

Look for the
hidden beauty in every day

I watched the sunlight casting rainbow patterns on the window pane.
It held my gaze for a while,
and I was grateful for that.
These little things that life gifts us, often go unnoticed.
But for one who is searching for a
segment of relief from the pain that pierces her heart ...
these moments are precious.

GRIEF IS A SHAPE SHIFTER

Grief I have found is like a shape shifter
It morphs and changes
sometimes on a daily, or even an hourly basis.
When I asked Grief about this she told me to just go with the flow.
She told me not to try to change things.
Just to accept whatever was arising in that moment.
To remain detached (if I could)..... and just observe.
It took some practice in the beginning,
but I have found, in doing this,
the emotions pass through me and eventually melt away.....
Grief tells me....
It's OK to feel sad
It's also OK to feel joy
It's OK to miss my son, desperately
It's also OK not to think of him sometimes...
........and not to feel guilty about that! ...
because I used to...believe me!
It's OK to break down and cry until no more tears will come.
It's also OK to laugh until my sides hurt....
Tears and laughter, are equal agents of healing, grief says.
It's OK to retreat from the world and spend the day on my own.
It's also OK to go out into the big world and take my son with me,
so we can explore together.
It's OK to visit past memories that make me cry.
It's also OK to visit past memories that make me laugh!
It's OK to feel the full weight of the pain, knowing it won't break me.
It's also OK to feel great joy,
and should this feeling arise,
grief tells me to embrace it!
In fact Grief says that it's OK to feel EVERY emotion that arises,
be it pleasant or unpleasant,
because all feelings pass, sooner or later.
And they seem to pass sooner,
if I just surrender to them and allow them to be.

They are doing their job, Grief says...
They are healing a broken heart....

I got to thinking one day about what we leave behind after we are 'gone'.
Now that my son had finished his time on earth,
just what is it I wondered,
that each of us leaves behind when we exit this lifetime.

What do I want to leave behind?
What will my legacy be, when I return home to spirit?
This is something we seldom think about.
We are often too busy getting on with life...
getting by so to speak.
But grief has made me realise that life is precious
and so is the way we live it....
And the legacy we leave behind....matters.
Tomorrow isn't guaranteed to any of us,
yet we mostly live our lives as if it were.
To live life more consciously,
more aware of how our lives are impacting or could impact others,
not just those closest to us,
but those we've yet to meet...and those perhaps we'll never meet......
isn't that something to ponder?
Isn't that something worth thinking about?
On that particular day, I felt it was.

So I began to look at my son's life in this context.
From the outside, his life sure looked chaotic and disorganised at times.
But since his passing, I've begun to understand that it was far from what it seemed.
Kindness was always at the heart of everything he did.
He always saw the good in others, even when they were less than kind to him.
He also helped others to see the goodness in themselves.
This earned you the title of "legend" by his friends.

My son I feel, has woven kindness into the lives of others....
I see it in his brother and his sister...
I recognise it in myself.
He has, looking back now,
always been our North Star, even if we didn't always recognise it.
And he will continue to be our guiding light,
until we join him back home.

So it is with sincere gratitude, I say thank you to him,
for gracing our lives with his gentle presence,
and for weaving his unique quality of kindness, into our hearts.

Some way along my journey with grief,
I began to question whether I could find some 'meaning' in this loss of mine.
I'd read about 'post traumatic growth'
and I was sure I had experienced it myself too.

So when something challenging arises in my life now,
(or in the lives of those around me), I find my mind drifts to the question ...
Is there something more than meets the eye here?
Is there something in this experience, that can be learnt or understood ?

It hasn't always that way. I used to look at life's challenges and think
how awful...that seems so unfair... why would this be allowed to happen,
or why is this happening to me?

Now, when I look back on my life...on those life-changing events that rocked my world,
(and there have been quite a few),
I find deeper questions arise in my mind, like...
What wisdom was available in that event, for my ever-evolving soul?
What important life lessons, if any, did I learn?

When we begin to question our own experience of 'loss',
we may, if we choose, move into a space of expanded awareness ...
into a deeper understanding of life and death.
Wisdom, previously hidden from view, can rise to the surface.
It seems it has always been there, yet we had no reason to seek it, until now.

Grief has helped me to understand that our soul is intuitively guided through life.
And when challenges arise, understanding that we have access to this guidance system,
can be enormously helpful, as well as comforting.

There are many books available, that can teach us how to access our innate wisdom....
and I have read a lot of them !
I have also found, that sitting quietly and just asking, often gives me the answers I seek.
The answers may not come immediately, but they come eventually.

Embracing the answers we receive, takes some practice,
especially if it calls for a big shift in our 'belief system'.

Sometimes the 'meaning' that can be found in 'loss',
is a shift to a deepest understanding
that the Soul is eternal.....
........and there really is no 'death' at all.

This journey is teaching me....
It's important to have a positive outlook
and at the same time
it's important to honour our grief.

I spoke with grief one day while we sat next to a meandering river
in the warm spring sunshine, a year or so into my journey with her.
She explained to me that the way I experience this 'loss' of mine will change over time.
To begin with, she said, it will feel like being on a roller-coaster,
and this can last for quite some time, but eventually she said,
it will become more of a riverboat ride.

I've always loved the idea of a riverboat, and as we were sat beside a river,
it seemed appropriate that I ask her how this was possible.
Again, she spoke of acceptance.
I kept hearing that concept arise.
In the beginning, acceptance was difficult.
But I had accepted pretty much at least, that I couldn't change the 'reality' I found myself in.
My son had left this world, and although I couldn't 'believe it' at first,
I had no choice but to accept it was true.

Even so, the 'reality' of it can still hit me like a ton of bricks even after 4 years
and I am back on that roller-coaster ride, having the wind knocked out of me.
But grief was right.
Nowadays, life is more like riding a riverboat.
I'm not in control of my destination, but the ride is less frantic,
less surprising and dare I say, more enjoyable?

The fact that I am not in control of my destination,
is something this journey with grief has been teaching me these last few years.
I used to believe that I had control of things, but that was in my younger, more naive days.

My son, while he was here on earth, taught me that no matter what I did,
I couldn't control the outcome of his destiny. A BIG lesson, but an important one.

Now on my riverboat ride with grief, I happily leave the steering to a higher power than me.
I've learnt to trust that life will take me where I need to go.

Relinquishing control isn't always easy,
neither is acceptance,
but I've come to embrace both,
and learning to trust in the process,
has changed my experience of life,
from a roller-coaster ride,
to a more enjoyable riverboat cruise.

Our loved ones often send us butterflies,
dragonflies and birds, to let us know they are near.
This beautiful little robin hopped onto my knee
as I sat in the park on my birthday,
then stayed with me for half an hour,
even eating from my hand.

Today my heart is filled with joy
for no apparent reason.
It's a beautiful feeling
and I accept it graciously
and without question.

Times like these were rare in the early days
but they are becoming more common.
I embrace every opportunity to feel joy.
Just as grief can arise for no apparent reason,
so it seems can joy.
Another reminder of the ups and downs
and mysteries of life...

Joy

Keep reminding yourself often,
that your loved ones don't leave you,
they simply change form.
When we drop our physical body,
we begin a new chapter of our lives.
It is not hard for them to reach us,
though we may have a hard time at first,
sensing their presence.
Just know that they are always near,
whether we can feel them or not.
I know that my son often feels closer to me now,
than when he was in his physical form.
We are <u>always</u> surrounded by,
and showered with,
the unconditional love of those in spirit.
Sit and bathe in that love, often.
By doing so,
you will learn to recognise the unique energy
of your loved one.

Difficult days to navigate...

When we are missing someone we love from our life,
certain days can be especially difficult for us.
New Year for a lot of grieving people, can be an immense challenge.
We often have the misconception that we are somehow
leaving our loved ones behind as we enter a new year...
as if we ever would...or could!
No.
They come with us wherever we go.
We carry them in our hearts from one year into the next...
When I was facing the first new year after my son's passing
and I was experiencing downward spiralling thoughts,
I heard my son whispering to me...
'I'm right there with you, Mum....Where else would I be'.
I have come to understand as I travel this journey,
that if I pay attention and watch my thoughts,
I can see how some thoughts or misconceptions,
send me swiftly on a downward spiral, and others, can be uplifting.
So I decide to make a conscious effort daily, to choose uplifting thoughts.
Granted, it isn't always easy.... or possible.
In the beginning I had to make this conscious effort many times a day.
Nowadays, it seems to be becoming second nature to me.
I am slowly learning the art of 'watching my thoughts,
and changing them, not just from negative to positive,
but questioning the validity of the thought itself...
I ask questions like...
Can I look at this differently? Is this thought serving me? Is it even true?
Grief reminds me that this is a healing practice to adopt.

I have now entered a few 'New Years', with my son spirit side,
and he always reminds me of the same things....
That I not only survived the last year,
but I did so, with more love and compassion in my heart.
I am much more conscious in each passing year, of my own suffering
and how grief affects me and I am also more conscious of the suffering of others too.
I am also more conscious of all of the healing that has gone on during the previous year.
I enter each New Year with the gift of love, hope and gratitude in my heart
and I thank the previous year, for the strength and wisdom it bestowed upon me.
Love, along with grief, seems to have taken root in my heart,
and for that, I am grateful.

Heart opens
Heart feels
Heart trusts
Heart yields

Heart breaks
Heart burns
Heart wanes
Heart learns

Heart closes
Heart sleeps
Heart awakens
Heart seeks

Heart opens
Heart knows
Heart heals
Heart grows

Our loved ones are always listening....

I saw you crying today.
I felt your emotions before the tears
had a chance to fall
and I was at your side...
I know you felt my presence.
I can sense when you do.
Even when the air is thick with the heaviness of grief
I am right beside you,
absorbing some of the pain.
These times we are together,
I can tell you so much about life..
So much about joy and laughter
amid the pain of a human existence.
There truly is, a time to laugh and a time to cry.
Both equal to one another.
All beautiful expressions of human emotions
that we come here to experience and explore.
Please don't ever judge yourself.
There is no judgement here.
Just a gentle acceptance of what is.
Allow your heart to guide the way.
She is your own unique vessel of love
that you can dip, or dive into,
whenever you need to.
Place your hands over her often,
and feel her warmth.
She holds immense energy reserves
which are at your disposal.
Connect with your heart
Connect with your soul
Allow love to expose the heaviness of grief
and drown it with her light.

Storm clouds are gathering

The storm-clouds are gathering up ahead
I can feel them in the distance
looming
gaining strength
their ominous presence approaching
like an unwelcome visitor.
It's as if they sense....
these days of such significance ...
Birth-days
Anniversary of the day you left
Anniversaries of times that are meaningful...
memories that can't be erased,
that I wish not to erase,
from the calendar of our life together.

So face them I must
and I will.
For you remind me that I am as powerful as any storm.
I can match its intensity,
and embrace these days
and reclaim them as my own,
until they hold no power to bring me down
but lift me up in celebration of you.

And I will celebrate these days
with love
with devotion
with YOU...

.....and with Banoffee pie, I hear you add !!

Can one ever be free of grief?

I don't know the answer to this question, at the time of writing,
but I expect the answer is no.... Not entirely.
Grief is a natural response to the 'death' of someone we dearly love.
And of course, I loved my son dearly, and still do,
so it stands to reason that grief in some shape or form,
will always be there.
And that's OK.
I've learned over time, to accept grief as my friend.
She certainly turned out to be very wise, once I got to know her.
She let's me know if something is going to be too painful to handle
and she advises me what to do instead.
She lets me know when to cry buckets of tears
that need to be released.
and she sits with me, whilst I do "just that".
I have learned to love and respect her
and I know she does the same for me.

And I discovered something else about this grief of mine,
which has turned out to be very important to me.
My son's spirit is entwined in this grief.
And I have come to fully trust my son,
to show me how to travel this road.

Grief is not the enemy I once thought she was.
Grief is a natural response to loss.
Grief is often.... though not always, hard work.
Sometimes she is soft, like raindrops
on a summer afternoon,
bringing relief when needed.

Embracing grief has been fundamental
in my quest to heal this broken heart of mine.
And I know it's possible to heal from great pain.....
I'm doing it.

I made a conscious decision in the early days, to try my best to heal.
A decision I felt it necessary for me to make, if I was to survive my son's death.
It took, and still can take, enormous effort some days...... but that's OK.

The alternative is far too painful to imagine.

I didn't smile much in the early days.
I found it really difficult and I would often avoid
people's gaze, keeping my eyes downcast.
But I love smiling at people now.
I love to see their faces change and light up,
as they smile back.
Perhaps no one has smiled at them for a long time....

Some don't smile back of course,
but that's OK.
Maybe they are having a hard time
and didn't have a smile to give away that day,
so at least they got one of mine.

I know how hard it can be to smile when one is in deep sorrow.
It somehow won't form on your lips.

But grief told me to try it one day.
She said no matter how I was feeling,
just to put a little smile on my face
and see if I could feel the difference.

One day I was really agitated about something
and I heard her words,
encouraging me to smile.
'You can't continue being agitated
and have a smile on your face', she said...
and she was right.
I smiled and my agitation just melted away.

I practice smiling a lot more these days.....

Watching you....

I watch you with eyes overflowing with love,
from my home inside the vastness of the cosmos,
among the stars that shine a thousand lights upon you, unseen.

I watch you bending to pick up the pieces of your broken heart
instinctively knowing that nothing must be left behind...
aware in some fledgling part of your new and emerging reality,
that everything holds value.

I watch you as you lovingly embrace that part of yourself
that still remains broken by my parting,
knowing without searching, that she needs this.
Knowing that that broken part of you,
requires your own unique blend of 'kintsugi' love
to put her back together again,
in a way she will be transformed by the golden hues of Grace.

I watch you from my place of beauty, with breathtaking love,
piecing your life back together in a beautiful kaleidoscope of patterns
and I notice with a heart filling with pride,
that the picture that is being created,
the sculpture you are crafting,
the image that is coming into focus,
holds so much purity, so much love,
so much to share.

I watch you from my place of peace,
among the slow, tranquil movement of others around me....
......others who watch over their own loved ones every day,
with the same care, pride, devotion and love as I give you.
And I smile with gratitude, that I knew you as you were,
that I know you as you are,
and I recognise who you are becoming....
For believe me when I tell you...
...you are a thing of beauty in a world that needs so much more...

Keep going....
the path you are forging behind you, is catching the attention of starlight
and merging with the spirit of love, hope,
and remembering of who we really are ...
and what we came here to do.

Remember....Our loved ones are not gone from our lives.
They are on a journey with us.
A <u>very special</u> journey.
One that we can't fully understand
while we are still in this human body.
But if we embrace the mystery of it all...
if we embrace the 'not knowing' where it will take us,
we may be in for a
beautiful, breathtaking ride!!

Life's journey...a metaphor for facing life with and 'without you'

Our journey begins when we are born and our parents are already on the train.
At various stages, people get on and others leave the train of life.
Some we miss when they depart and others...we hardly notice their absence at all.

We know in the back of our mind...though we rarely think about it,
that one day, we will reach OUR stop... and we will leave the train ....
We all do.
But what about what we do in-between boarding and stepping off the train?
Isn't that what really counts, no matter how long the journey is?
Be it a moment, a few years, or decades...?
I began to question this metaphor of the train journey.
What is it that we are doing between stops?
Is your journey an exhilarating ride, where you speed along and the scenery is ever changing
with colourful contrasts and you hardly pause for breath, before you are on to the next new bright light,
calling you from up ahead? (this is what my son's journey looked like to me).
Or is your journey much more serene,
where you explore deeply everything you see from the window, as you slowly move along?
(this is more how I see my journey)
Do you sometimes wish your train would slow down...or speed up?
Or that the scenery would be different tomorrow,
from what it has been today, or last week, last month, or last year?

Do you wish you could get off at a station that isn't yours,
but someone else's...someone you love? (I know I did).
Do you wish you could experience their reality... for a while at least,
before they disappear into the mist that lies beyond their station,
and they enter their next adventure?

What is your onward journey like, when someone gets off the train
when you didn't expect them to?
When unexpected things happen in life, what is it that you do?
Do you hide in the luggage compartment perhaps, and stop looking out of your window?
Do you stop appreciating the view?
Do you feel your journey is also over,
and you have lost all interest, in what lies ahead?
The thing is....it may just be the most beautiful 'view' you've ever encountered !
It may turn out to be the most incredible chapter of your life !

And you will never know.... unless you get back in your seat....

Follow the subtle signs your body is sending you.
It will let you know if it wants to laugh, or cry, or be silent.
If it wants to be in company, or alone.
Do this your own way...It's your grief.
Others can give advice and say what they found helpful
and if it resonates with you, give it a try.
But remember, there's no right or wrong way to grieve.....
Give yourself permission to do it your way.
And your way may change as time goes by.
Listen to what your body and soul are telling you.
They both know the way.
Listen to and learn to trust that small voice within.
And remember, wherever you are on your journey
Be gentle on yourself...

YOU'RE DOING OK
AND THAT'S MORE THAN ENOUGH

Grief reminds me that not all days are the same.
Some days I can feel strong and my mind
tricks me into thinking I am 'getting there',
as if '<u>there</u>' is a better destination than here.
I found this difficult to navigate,
especially in the early days, but later on in the journey, too.
For instance,
I can feel like I am doing fine.
Life is enjoyable and for a moment or two
I 'forget' that I am 'grieving'.
Life seems to flow along like a sweet song.
Then I will wake up one morning and
the 'realisation' that my son has died, hits me like a ton of bricks,
and a whole new ocean of tears opens up inside of me.
Grief tells me that all of this is natural
and not just natural, but necessary.
She tells me that down in the hidden depths
are emotions that I have pushed down,
not just relating to my son's death,
but emotions that have been denied
from earlier life experiences too.
The body, she tells me,
is an amazing instrument
(and I am only beginning to realise, just how amazing it is)
and, she says,
it knows how to cleanse and heal itself,
but all too often, *we* get in the way.
There are things that we may have been told in the past,
or picked up from the culture around us, a chance remark etc.
and it is sitting in our psyche and we are often
responding unconsciously from that place.
We may have been told it is weak to cry,
that we should hide our emotions etc.
or we may feel if we really let it all out,
we may never stop!
But if we hold back, when we feel the need to release,
our body will seek to take over.
I have been learning to trust grief for a while now,
and I am beginning to trust the innate wisdom of my body too.
So now, when I feel the tears forming,
I give them my time ... and I give them the space they need.

We can get so caught up in the current of life,
that we miss what life has to offer us.
Today, try to consciously slow down.
Listen out for the gentle voice of your loved one
in the silence that they create...for the both of you.
It can become a natural thing to do....
It IS natural, but somehow, we have forgotten.

Take some time each day ......
just 5 minutes to begin with,
to sit with your loved one
and give them your full, undivided attention.
We would do this naturally, if they were in bodily form,
so why not do it in spirit form?
See how it feels.
Really take in and explore the energy between you.
Talk to them.
They are right next to you....eager to connect.

This morning,
I opened the window to my heart
I felt her tenderness, as well as her strength
blending like a gracious lover with my vulnerability.
Seeping slowly into the jagged brickwork of the stronghold I had erected,
and fortified over a lifetime, as a protection against the ravages of life.
I opened the window to my heart this morning,
so that all the love that dwelt therein could come rushing out,
to bathe me in the warm balm of her comforting embrace,
... a loyal friend,
who is always there...
watching...
waiting for an invitation to provide a soft place to land,
should I stumble and fall at life's many hurdles.
I opened the window to my heart this morning
and she shone her wondrous light upon me and I was captured in her beam,
like the elusive snow leopard,
a rare beauty, reflected in the camera lens ....
contrasting with the darkness of the night.
I opened the window of my heart this morning
and I rose with the freedom of a feather
to an altered state of being,
to an unfamiliar frequency,
where great symphonies serenaded one another in an exquisite melody,
that brought the angel choir down from heaven to listen to the sacred sound.
I opened the window to my heart this morning
and I saw myself...for the first time
a beautiful fragile, strong, wise, forgotten woman
who has been waiting all along...patiently
for a time to be free
I opened the window to my heart this morning
and we merged together, she and I, like pieces of a puzzle waiting to be solved.
I opened the window to my heart this morning,
and she showed me what I'd denied myself all these years
and when I accepted all she had to offer me...
her grace
her beauty
her love
I was complete.
This morning, I opened the window to my heart
and I vowed not to close it again....

The sea is choppy this morning,
washing over the rocks depositing white foam
before retreating back to build up strength once again.
I notice, as I sit looking out at the horizon,
how a different picture is painted on the landscape each day.
Earlier in the week, the sea was calm, like a serene lake,
reflecting the welcoming rays of the midday sun
and the somewhat unusual colour of the turquoise sky.
Today, the grey of the clouds is the only colour reflected in the
choppy waters.

I watch a lone surfer out in the distance,
and I wonder how they manage to remain upright,
with the force of the waves driving them along.

'It's because they've learnt to ride them', grief whispers.
'They've fallen many times no doubt,
but they're never too discouraged,
not to get back up again and keep trying....
Just like you'.

I smiled.
Grief knows just what to say.

Holding on and Letting go

I didn't realise I was holding on so tightly until I released the grip
on the arm of the chair on which I was sitting.
Tense, ever so tense,
my body had fallen into this pattern and weaved
its own intricate design to fulfil the intention I'd unconsciously built
..... of holding on.....
But relax, the voice on the recording urged....
Relax and let go.
I took in another deep breath as instructed and breathed out with a sigh.
Was this working?
What was I doing this for?
Shouldn't I be doing something more constructive with my time,
instead of sitting here, trying to relax?
Shouldn't I be building an empire in your memory...
or painting the town with a dazzling display of
your kindness and grace?
'No,' a voice whispered.
'No need at this moment, for grand gestures ....
just relax'.
A warmth embraced me and I knew you were present.
I had come to know that familiar feeling you bring with every visit.
I had come to know your essence, through hours of sitting like this.
Devoting my time not just to you, but to myself, too.
Tending to the part of me that is grieving.

Time enough for building empires and spreading kindness, I thought
and I felt you agree.

'Spending time together is building something far more valuable', you said.
'It's building and strengthening the connection between us'.

Today I awoke with that familiar heavy feeling inside of me.
I had felt it a bit yesterday, as the day went on.
When I awoke this morning, it greeted me.
It's a familiar feeling now, but I still call it an
'unwelcome visitor'.
So I sat down to have a conversation with Grief
and I asked her..."why am I feeling this way today?"
'Does it matter why'? she replied.
"Yes", I said
'Why does it matter'? she asked
"Because if I know what's caused it, I can try to fix it."
As I said these words, a realisation came
and I felt grief smiling kindly beside me.
'You always want to fix things don't you', she said gently.
"Yes...I suppose I do".
"Is there any reason why I shouldn't?" I asked.
'Grief isn't something you can fix', she said.
'It's a process that leads to understanding'.
"So what do I do when I feel like this?" I asked.
'Just allow your feelings to be there'..she said
'You just allow them to be.....
and in time, they will pass, like they always do....'

One sunny afternoon, I was given a wonderful gift from a stranger.
I met a lady, while queuing for coffee in a country park.
The queue was quite long as we joined it together and she started chatting, telling me
she was having a break from caring for her elderly Mum, and was on holiday in the area
with her daughter. We talked about the difficulties having aged parents brings,
then, as so often happens, she asked me if I had any children.
I felt my hesitation. That moment of not knowing exactly what to say.
"Yes, I have 3," I answered. My youngest son passed away in 2019,
so I have 2 this side of life and one spirit side.
She didn't miss a beat with her next question.
"How do you feel about that?" she asked.
Again, I hesitated. I wasn't used to being asked that question by anyone, least of all a stranger.
"It hasn't been easy, but I have my faith in the afterlife, so that helps", I said.
"How did it happen, if you don't mind me asking?" was her next question.
Again....that hesitation...What would I say?
Was I open to having my son judged?
He'd been judged often enough during his lifetime and I didn't want him judged in death, also.
It was something I knew I struggled with ... this need to protect him.
But at the same time I knew that there should be no shame, or judgement in how my son left this earth.
"It was an accidental overdose", I said.
"Oh I'm sorry," she replied...."Was he unhappy?"
"Life wasn't always easy for him," I said.
She smiled, kindly..."It can't have been easy for either of you."
"No," I replied, "but because of my faith and belief that he's now free of suffering,
I'm managing to cope the best I can.
And also, I feel his spirit and know he's always watching over me", I said.
I didn't often share my belief in the spirit world with strangers, but .....
She nodded and smiled. "I know something of how you feel", she continued.
"My son died in 2002, at 14 yrs of age.
"Oh I'm sorry" I said...."so you do know......"
"Yes," she said.....
"How did you cope?" I asked.
"Same as you", she said...."With my faith and belief in the afterlife".
We talked for a while longer about our sons and their fun-loving personalities and kind nature.
Seems they had much in common.
We were two strangers, sharing a sacred bond... and as we went our separate ways
and I sat in a beautiful spot to drink my coffee,
I realised that this lady had given me a beautiful gift.
She had allowed me to talk about my son and his passing
and she was truly interested and coming from a place of love.
Sadly, this freedom to speak openly about death and grief and the world of spirit, is quite rare.

Look to Nature for answers

We all need a little extra support at times.

In my conversations with Grief
she reminds me that this journey should be thought of
more like a marathon, than a sprint.
There is no need to feel you have to to rush things, she says,
..... to reach some imaginary finish line.
.....In truth, there isn't one.
She tells me this not to make me sad,
but rather to wake me up to the fact
that I don't have to pressurise myself.....
to do better...
to be better...
I can simply be where I am,
on any given day,
or in any given moment.
She reminds me gently,
that nature goes through cycles...
through seasons.
Nature blooms and blossoms at certain times
and seems to hibernate at others.
And yet, even in hibernation,
things are happening,
under the surface...unseen.
She tells me that nature takes care of its own
and likewise,
I too, am being taken care of.
She tells me to look to nature and see this for myself.
Nature doesn't strive for anything.
Nature takes its own course, she says.
And so too, grief needs to be free to do the same.
She tells me to be patient with myself.
Nothing in nature blooms all year round.

Living Peacefully

I have often wondered what it would be like,
to Live Peacefully.
It certainly sounds a wonderful thing to do, or place to be.
But what does it mean?
We will all have our own ideas, or perceptions of
what it may mean to live peacefully, and I think I would be
correct in saying, that we would certainly all _like_ to
have a peaceful life.
Is it possible for Grief and Peace, to live alongside one another?
Absolutely YES,
in my experience they can.
Do I feel in a peaceful state all day every day?
Certainly not.
When grief comes calling and tears are streaming down my face
and my cries can be heard by the neighbours,
I am certainly feeling far from peaceful.
But once the tears subside, I know I will return to
a sense of inner peace.
A resting place in my heart has been created.
Carved out of hours of meditation,
contemplation, understanding,
and often sheer hard work.
Yes, grief can be hard work!
But those moments of peace that I am finding more often lately....
are a welcome balm to my suffering.
They are what I like to call 'God's Grace.'
They are there to show me that even in the midst of grief,
Grace is always there,
waiting for an opening, an opportunity,
to show herself.
When I am fully with Grace, I feel at peace.

Mind the one you feed

There is a legend, believed to be Cherokee in origin, about two wolves.
Perhaps you've heard it, perhaps not.
It goes like this....

A wise old Cherokee is teaching his grandson about life.
"A fight is going on inside us," he says to the boy.
'What sort of fight, Grandfather?' the boy asks.
"It's like a fight between two wolves", says the wise old man.
"One is full of anger, envy, guilt, resentment,
and ego.
The other is full of joy, peace, love, humility,
kindness, compassion and faith.
The same fight is going on inside of you – and inside of me.
It's a fight that is going on inside every person who walks this earth,"
he says to the boy.
The boy looked up at his wise old grandfather and asked...
"Which one wins Grandfather?"
"The one you feed" said the wise man...
"The one you feed".

I came across this story a long time ago and it has always stuck with me.
In my journey with grief, I have applied the wisdom from this teaching,
many times....and still do.

Our thoughts are more powerful than we often realise.
They can lift us up, only to drag us down in a heartbeat!

It's empowering to know, we have a choice in every moment,
which thoughts to embrace
....and which ones to let go of.

Grief reminds me to feed the thoughts that bring me peace,
joy, humility and all the other virtues
that are helping me along life's path.

Another loss....

In August 2021,
my mother had a fall
which ultimately
led to her passing...
She was just shy of her
90th birthday
She sends me
forget-me-nots
as a way of letting
me know,
she's near.

A forget me not in a flower pot
reminding me of you...
Strong, yet fragile.
Growing with a simplistic beauty all of her own
She does not strive or strain
She meets the sunlight or shadow with equal gaze
Her only requirement of me is liquid love
that I pour through a tiny spout
into the soil in which she dwells.
We are one, she and I
She provides me with beauty, I provide her with love.
A simple yet profound exchange.
One day, she will leave.
Her flowers once so charming to my eye
will wither along with her leaves
reminding me not to hold on
but to let go
and remember
the joy she brought to my life
for the time she was here.
Just like you......

She looked so small in that hospital bed,
like a child, who had progressed too soon from crib to toddler bed.
Her complexion was as pale as the stark white sheets that were tucked around her shoulders, hiding the fragile body, bruised by the fall.
She'd never been a big lady, and she'd shrunk further in her later years
and now, lying there, she was but a shadow of the vibrant woman I remember from my youth.
She had been drifting in and out of consciousness
just as I had been drifting in and out of sleep.
The hours were long at that bedside but I didn't want to miss a moment
of this time I had been gifted with her.
In truth, she could have left the moment that she had fallen,
but her resilience, determination and sheer grit that she'd built her life upon,
gave her the strength to raise the alarm, so she could spend
these last precious days with her family.....And I admired her for that.
I didn't think it was possible to love her any more than I already did.
But hearing of her courageous hours of struggle from the garden, to raise the alarm
with what she called God's angel choir playing in the background, urging her on,
touched my heart in a way it hadn't been touched before.
So here we were, her and I, mother and daughter, roles reversed,
in the early morning hours, before the sun put in its appearance for the day.
When all was silent, save the occasional footsteps in the hallway
and the constant drip, drip, drip of the machine that fed her body with essential nutrients,
attempting to sustain life that little bit longer.
I knew my son Dan was in the room with me.
I'd asked him to help me to be present with my mother
throughout these next however many
hours or days, before she made her journey home.
I felt his energy move beside me in the solemn atmosphere of the hospital room.
That familiar tingle down the right hand side of my face,
like he was kissing the air around me.
My mother was teaching me about life and death in that hospital room we shared.
She had woken from her sleep state a few days earlier
and with eyes still closed,
announced with a faint smile, just about visible behind her oxygen mask,
that she'd seen God.
'God has a lovely face', she said. 'A lovely face and a lovely nature'.
Did you really see God?, I asked
She answered with slow but emphatic nod of her head.
'Did you see anyone else', I asked and without giving her a chance to answer....
'Did you see Dan?'

cont...

She smiled again, no doubt knowing how important her words were to me.
A pause ...'Yes, I saw Dan and I saw my mother and father and my sister Betty.'
Her words entered like sunlight to nourish my weary Soul, lighting me up from the inside,
warming my heart, so it beat that little bit faster than its normal rhythm.
And with that, she drifted back to wherever she had been
and the smile settled on her lips and I knew she was content in her knowing
and any fears she may have held about death had evaporated,
like raindrops touching the parched landscapes of the desert, unseen by the human eye.
She knew...... And I relaxed back into the imitation leather hospital chair
with its unyielding straight back and smiled along with her....
'her knowing', strengthening my own.
The sun began to rise and I knew that this quiet solitude we shared, would disappear
along with the darkness, as another day in the hospital ward was ushered into life.
A gentle knock at the door, a friendly face offering a smile...
'Would you like a cup of tea'?
I nodded as she glanced toward my mother....'Did she have a good night?'
I nodded again as she closed the door as silently as she could, behind her.
Soon the peaceful atmosphere that had settled in the room,
was put away for the day with the arrival of the cleaner.
He was dressed in a maroon uniform, distinguishing him from the rest of the staff.
He said a cheery good morning,
and I felt his warmth and answered as cheerily as I could.
He was a big man...Tall and muscular, with jet black hair and a complexion
that appeared to have weathered many of life's challenges.
But it was the enormous cross that I was drawn to.
It hung from his neck like a medallion of honour I couldn't help but admire it.
'I love your cross and chain', I said to him,
as I lifted my feet off the floor, so he could manoeuvre the oversized mop into the corners.
His face lit up! ' Thank you', he said.
It was obvious he was proud of this piece of precious jewellery.
'I bought it in my home country and I bought the biggest one I could afford,
because I wanted to be reminded that the love of God is HUGE!'
He put down his mop and emphasised the word HUGE by spreading his arms
as wide as he could.
'I love God', he said as he picked up the mop to carry on his work.
'Me too', I said and he smiled........knowingly.
As he was leaving the room I said...."Its been lovely talking to you, what's your name?"
'DAN', he said, pointing to his name badge that I hadn't noticed until now.
'My name is Dan and it's been lovely talking to you too. God bless you.'
And he left me sitting there thanking my son for every precious sign he sends me,
and for what he does best....letting me know he always hears me and responds.

Has the impact of the death of my mother
been softened somehow,
because I've endured the passing of my son?
This is a question I ponder
as I feel an acceptance come over me
of the grand order of things.
An understanding that every person,
every event,
every birth
every death,
is contained within a perfect Universe,
and we move and dance and sway in time to its rhythm.
Is one death easier to bear than another?
I can't answer that.
Each death we endure, is unique in the way it affects us,
in a same way that each relationship is unique.
My mother holds a special place in my heart,
as she joins my son in spirit.

Learning to dance

I'm learning how to dance.
I'm learning how to dance with life
with death
with grief
with pain
with sorrow.
I'm learning how to dance with love,
with laughter.
with joy.
with carefree abandon.
I'm learning how to dance with life.
I am learning to "Dance with Dan".
He has so much to teach me,
from up in his ivory tower,
(which is how I sometimes lovingly refer to his heavenly home.)
He loved to dance when he was on earth.
Not the foxtrot, or slow waltz... No.
His own style of dance...
which may have appeared rather erratic
from the fleeting viewpoint of a passerby.
But if you'd looked closely enough,
he would have shown you
that he danced
to the music of the Soul...
HIS Soul!
And that's what he asks me to do.
To listen to my heart when she speaks ....
To hear her gentle melody playing a song from ancient times,
calling me back to myself.
So I listen...
and I hear...
and I learn...
and slowly...
I dance.

Just as a butterfly
struggles to emerge from her cocoon,
and the baby chick from its egg,
so we also struggle,
to emerge from grief
into the light of
our own healing
where we come to a deeper understanding
of the dance of life and death.

Grief brings transformation

I am in a period of transformation.
I am growing my wings.
They are translucent, delicate,
like the fine lace found on a handkerchief belonging to a Duchess, or Marquise.
They feel a little odd at the moment like they don't belong to me,
and they itch a little too if I'm honest,
but I'm told not to scratch them, lest I damage their gentleness,
their delicateness...their beauty.
I'm not sure I've earned these wings,
and I argue sometimes that they've been given to me by mistake,
like a mysterious package that arrived in the mail,
delivered to the wrong address ... awaiting return.
But they are mine, I'm told, so I'd best get used to them.
When I walk out with my wings they are of course,
invisible to others
but I feel them gently flapping about
like a baby bird, unsure of venturing from the
security of the mother's nest.
Gently they move back and forth,
as if gearing themselves up for something.
What? I'm unsure
but I'm told to trust.....so I do.
I know there are others with wings who walk where I walk.
Walking with wings unseen.
Some have grown into their wings
like a beautiful pair of fairy-tale slippers
made for a princess.
And we recognise them,
those with wings, who speak and act as if they
have come from heaven above to walk among us,
to teach us how to be,
how to love in this world,
in spite of life's difficulties.
We recognise them.
Our hearts open spontaneously when we are in their company.
We _all_ have these buds of wings eager to unfurl.
We _all_ have the potential to allow them to sprout and grow.
Mine, I'm tentatively trying them out..
How about you ?

Love is eternal

Experiencing Joy

I didn't expect to feel joy again, after you left.
I didn't expect to laugh at someone's silly joke.
I didn't expect to look forward to new things...
new adventures...new projects, or long lazy summer days.
I didn't expect to look forward to life!
I didn't expect to awaken in the early morning without
that old familiar feeling of dread
knocking on the doors and windows of my mind.
I didn't expect to embrace the brand new day before me
and feel excited about how I was going to fill it.
I didn't expect to feel joy.....
But I did.
It crept up on me, unexpectedly and surprised me with its presence.
It felt good.
Like finding a welcome place to shelter, from the blistering heat of the midday sun,
or sinking into a warm bubble bath, when your muscles are aching
from a challenging hike in the mountains.
IT FELT GOOD!
At first my mind told me I shouldn't be feeling this way.
"How can you feel happy when you're meant to be grieving?"
The cruel voice of my inner critic, wagged its sharp pointy finger at me.
"No one feels happy when their loved one has gone!"
Joy....that unfamiliar and up until now elusive feeling, ran for cover
and left me clinging to that sinking feeling once again.
Guilt quickly joined in the solemn gathering.
Regret too, put in an appearance.
Soon all the negative emotions were jockeying for position
in the arena of my mind.
This happened time and time again...in the beginning.
Then grief came and softly spoke in my ear.
She told me that it was entirely possible to be
happy and grieving at the same time.
'One need not cancel out the other...there is room for both' she said.
She told me to silence the voice of that inner critic
and not to buy into the lies that it told.
'When dealing with thoughts that run amok in the mind', she said,
'remember the Cherokee tale of the two wolves, and
be mindful of the ones you feed'.

Following an emotional storm one morning,
I sat in meditation for guidance and it was my dear mother,
who came through to me with these words.
Grief is like a tinderbox of emotion
....capable of combusting at any time.

Looking back on life ...what would I tell my younger self?

If I could go back in time and speak to my younger self,
what would I choose to tell her about the life that was to come?
Would I hurriedly share the wisdom that has been gained from 60 plus years.
Would I tell her that things were not going to be easy.
That life was going to pull her out of this splendour of youth by her hair braids
and toss her about like a fairground ride
and leave her lost and breathless and gasping for air ?
Would I tell her that she is going to know the depths of despair
but that hidden in the folds of its cloth,
she'll discover treasures of exquisite beauty that no human eye can see?
Would I tell her to enjoy all of the adventures that come her way before things change
and to treasure each one, like precious fragments of sea glass
that are only found once in a lifetime?
Would I tell her to remember to stand up for herself and see her own worth,
even when others refuse to see it and try to blind it from her,
because they don't understand her beauty...or their own ?
Would I tell her that she is unique and not to ever lose
that gift of kindness, that she will need to wear,
like a thick coat of protection against the harshness of life to come?
Would I tell her to hold on to the joy of childlike laughter, like an anchor, a lifeline,
that will save her from drowning in times of despair?
Would I tell her to treasure each and every joyful moment of youth,
as those delicious memories will help to sustain her when things get rough?
Would I tell her not to weigh herself down with things that don't matter
and leave her arms free for the blessings that come her way,
lest she might miss the opportunity to carry them, too?
Would I tell her that life will not be what she thinks it will be,
that at times, she will feel she has been given a boat without a rudder,
that is not fit to sail out of shore, let alone sail a lifetime in ?
Would I tell her that she'll develop the tools to repair her vessel along the way
and make it seaworthy?
Would I tell her that she is a magnificent being,
who comes to know life through many different experiences and
that even on the darkest of days, she will always see the light?
Yes...this is what I would tell her ...
That even on the darkest of days...YOU,
my young, sweet, innocent self .... will always see the light.

I wish I could have been the perfect mother.
I wish I could have sheltered you
from the harshness of life,
.....sheltered you from yourself.
All those times you threatened to self-destruct,
I wish I could have lessened the pain for you,
when you felt as broken
and as helpless as I did.

I wish I could have whisked us both away
to a fairy-tale land of make-believe,
where life wasn't harsh and unyielding.
Where life wasn't full of challenges and pitfalls,
that open up without warning,
like sink-holes,
changing the landscape in an instant,
claiming many an unsuspecting casualty.

I wish I could have helped you see through my eyes,
how beautiful, talented and gifted you were.
I wish I could have helped you see
what you brought to this world
with your uniqueness,
your kindness,
your compassion,
your grace,
in a world that is burning.

I wish I could have helped you to understand
that the thoughts that ran rampant
like crazed looters through your mind,
stealing your joy and zest for life,
didn't belong to you....
that they weren't yours,
were not a measure of you,
that they weren't truthful...
they weren't honest.

cont...

cont...

I wish I could have held you that little bit longer
in a mother's embrace,
before the world got hold of you,
ripping you from my bosom like a sticky plaster
from an unhealed sore.

I wish I could have paved your way with promises
that you'd never falter or fall
at life's impossible hurdles.

I wish I could have equipped you
with an impenetrable armour,
so that life couldn't hurt your gentle soul,
so that others couldn't bring you to your knees
with brutal labels
that cut open your fragile heart
and made you bleed tears of shame.

I wish I could have protected you,
when life seemed impossible for you to bear,
when you endlessly searched
for a way out of the maze
of the madness and misery.

I wish I could have promised
that life would make sense in the long run,
in a way that you could see,
in a way that we could both comprehend.
I wish I could have saved you....

but maybe,
just maybe,
it is you, who is saving me....

<u>An Ode To Grief</u>

Grief I discovered, has many different faces....

A nguish
N ever-ending

O verwhelming
D ebilitating
E rratic

T urbulent
O verpowering

G rueling
R elentless
I nsidious
E xhausting
F erocious

****
<u>The other faces of Grief....</u>

A ssuring
N urturing

O pening
D edicated
E mpathetic

T ender
O mnipresent

G uiding
R adiant
I nspiring
E ncouraging
F aithful

One never knows which face will show up when,
but as my journey progresses, I have experienced more assurance,
more radiance, and more tenderness in her embrace.

Sometimes people have asked me how I can be so strong
and able to carry on with life, following my son's death.
If I could explain ... and if they had time to listen,
I believe it would sound something like this.....
I can tell myself a story of how my son is no longer here,
or I can remind myself that he never really left.
I can tell myself the story of a life cut short...that he left too soon,
or I can remind myself that he lived the exact number of days he came here to live.
I can tell myself a story of how drugs ruined his life,
or I can remind myself that he got to experience more in his short life,
than many do in 80 plus years.
I can tell myself the story that his life held no meaning,
or I can remind myself that the loving kindness he shared with others
will reverberate through the universe forever more.
I can tell myself the story, that I miss his physical presence,
or I can remind myself, that I feel him close to me every moment of the day...
as soon as I tune in, he's there.
I can tell myself the story that no mother should lose a child,
or I can remind myself that many mothers do, including both of my grandmothers.
I can tell myself the story that he will miss out on so many things he never got to do,
or I can remind myself that he got to do everything he came here to do.
I can tell myself the story that I will never get to see my son again,
or I can remind myself how wonderful the reunion will be, when I return home.
I can tell myself the story that my son is lost,
or I can remind myself that he dwells in a place of beauty, I can only dream of.
I can tell myself the story that life is cruel and harsh and there's no point in going on,
or I can open my eyes to the beauty and magic that is all around me
and embrace life and all it has to offer.
I choose the story (or the thoughts), that bring peace to my heart and soul.
I know my son would want it no other way.
His guidance and reassurance are deeply embedded in my bones.
I have worked at this....
In the early days, I had to choose a better story many times a day, now, it's less than once a week.
Maybe there will always be that voice that wants to draw me back into the darkness,
but the light of my son and the light of my own faith are so much stronger than that voice.
This is how I choose to live.
This is how I choose to survive and to thrive.
This is how I choose to honour my son and the choices we both made, a long time ago.
I choose to tell myself the story that brings peace to my heart.

This is what I would say to someone, if they ask me how I can be so strong....

Butterflies appear when loved ones are near

and even rhinos!

It was a Saturday in late September and I was on my way
to a psychic workshop in a nearby town.
I had seen the advert for the workshop a few weeks earlier and I had felt drawn to go.
I've gotten used to following these little nudges over the past few years.
As I was walking from the car park,
I was having a conversation in my mind with my son.
In fact, I was scolding him ...(all in good humour of course).
I belong to an online group for those who are grieving
and one of the things we do on a regular basis, is participate in something called,
'Sign of the Week'
The administrator of the group will put up a sign every Monday,
(usually an animal of some sort), and the idea is that
you ask your loved one to bring you that sign in some shape or form.
It is an excellent exercise to develop communication between you and
your loved one in spirit and Dan and I had been playing this game for quite some time.
The sign for that particular week was rhinoceros and as yet, I hadn't had one!
So as I was walking to the hall, I was scolding Dan and telling him
that he had better bring me my rhinoceros soon, as the week was almost over!

The workshop was full and the medium who was conducting the class,
was a lovely lady, who had given me a beautiful, evidential reading
just a few months after Dan passed to spirit.
We took a break for lunch and we all sat in a circle.
We had been instructed beforehand, to bring a packed lunch with us.
The medium taking the class, struck up a conversation with a gentleman sitting
opposite me, so it was easy to overhear what they were saying.

I almost laughed out-loud and nearly choked on my sandwich
when I heard the conversation.
It went like this...
Medium to the gentleman ... "Are you a vegetarian?"
Gentleman ... 'No, but I've recently given up eating rhinoceros'.
She looked at him surprised and he mumbled...
'I've no idea where that came from!'
When the workshop was over, I was able to enlighten him on exactly
what had made him say he'd given up eating rhinoceros...
My son!
We did have a good laugh about it and on the way back to the car,
I thanked Dan for his ingenious way of delivering 'sign of the week'!

Going through the grieving process,
is a bit like entering a maze.
You are shown the entrance,
but once you get inside,
there are so many twists and turns,
many obstacles that seem to be blocking your way,
you are continually searching for the right direction to go in.

But I have found that even the 'blind alleys'
that make you turn around and retrace our steps,
have something to teach us.
They encourage us to keep going,
learning along the way.

The walls of a maze are high enough
so we can't see over them.
We can't see the exit.
And it is the same with grief.

We enter a maze, knowing that eventually
we will come out the other end.... that we will find the exit point.
But grief doesn't seem to have an end.
There is no exit point as such.
But it does have many rest stops.
And it has .... and holds many clues to the unseen world.

Grief does offer us a treasure map
when we enter its maze.
And if we pay attention
as we travel along this journey of no definitive destination,,
we WILL be rewarded.
Not just at the end of this earthly life, but as we are living it too.

And remember,
our loved ones are with us...in this maze.
They can see the paths we need to take.
They offer us clues if we can but recognise them.
They can't deliver us from the maze we find ourselves in,
but they can ... and do, hold our hand all the way.

How does one survive deep grief?
I wondered at the beginning if indeed I would survive.
I remember wishing years away in those first few days.
Wishing I could wave a magic wand and years would have passed,
and I would be in a much better place, because the pain was unimaginable.
And now, four years on
I am reminded of just how swiftly time passes.
My son reminds me constantly not to waste time on anything that doesn't serve my Soul.
It's taken some effort, a great deal of effort if I'm honest....(and I'm still very much in the process,)
but today and most days, I'm doing OK.
The deep pain of grief is so much softer now and more bearable.
It has been replaced with a deep love and respect for my self and the strength and endurance
that I've encountered and integrated along the way.
I believe the resilience of the human spirit
is within us all in times of crisis.
When we come into these human bodies,
we are equipped with a capacity to endure.
I knew this more than mere words.
I felt it deep down in the centre of my being,
that I would not be given something
I couldn't live through.
I do sometimes wish that I hadn't had to walk this path,
and that my son was still here on earth, fit, healthy and living a happy life.
But life didn't work out that way and if I say I had to make the best of it, it sounds trite,
but in truth, I, like so many of us who travel this road of deep grief,
we have no other choice than to make some sort of sense from the wreckage of our lives.
I believe we all have the capacity to rise,
and emerge from the fire we've walked through,
and come out with more than we took in with us.

I remind myself of this, constantly.

My son Dan returned to spirit on April 30th 2019.
How could so much time have passed by already, is a questions I often ask myself?
Is this question it helpful?
Will I still be asking the same question 10 years from now?
Does thinking in terms of time, serve any real purpose?

How have I survived?
Another question I've asked myself, many times over.
And as I ask it again now,
I hear the familiar tone of Dan's voice as he says....
"You've survived well".

'You think so', I ask?
"Well, don't you?" comes his reply....
....followed by that familiar chuckle of his.
'I don't know', I say.
'It's certainly not been easy...
...It still isn't easy!'
"That could be up for debate", I hear him say.
And I know there is wisdom to be had here,
so I accept his invitation to debate the subject.

While in his earthly body,
Dan was often full of wisdom and nothing got by him easily.
He would question things a LOT, as a young child.
He was certainly never a conformist.
He was seldom argumentative in his approach,
he simply had a way that would make you question your assumptions.
And here he was....
doing the same again.

'But it hasn't been easy', I say again.
'And I think I've only survived with your help'.
"But you were never meant to go it alone", I hear him say.
"This was always going to be a joint effort.
All these years without my physical presence,
just the light of my love to guide your way....
And you've done it....
You got here.... You've survived."

cont....

cont...

"And what's more, you can go on into the future,
safe in the knowledge that I will always be by your side".
And as I hear these words, I KNOW that the light of his love
is what has got me through these past years.
For the light of his love has taught me, that the illusion of separation,
is only experienced through our five senses.
And just because I can't see him with my physical eyes,
doesn't mean he's not right here beside me.
And just because I can't hear him with my physical ears,
the same way I used to,
doesn't mean he's not speaking to me.
And just because I can't physically put my arms around him,
......(like I'd love to be able to do)
doesn't mean I can't feel and sense him when he's near.

The light of his love has taught me,
that there can be no separation between souls.
The light of his love has taught me,
that the 'illusion of separation' comes,
when we experience the 'loss' of a physical body.

But when we come to understand that the body is not who we are,
we also come to understand that we can be just as close,
if not closer, to our loved ones now,
whose true essence is 'all spirit'.
Because after all, that is our true essence too!
We just have to learn to shift our awareness
off the separation and onto the connectedness.

So that's what I'm doing.
And that is what I will continue to do,
to help me to move through whatever the future holds.
And I know that this allows me to honour this wonderful,
wise and caring companion of mine,
who keeps his promise to always be by my side.
And when I remember this,
I know I can survive however long I have left in this earthy realm.

This wasn't what I expected my life to turn out like.
This wasn't what I expected when I gave birth to this beautiful child,
full of sunny smiles and laughter.
But here we are.
This has been our journey.
Through grief, I have learned so much more about life.
More than I would have,
had Dan not left this earth and joined me on my spiritual journey.

Would I have consciously chosen this experience from a human perspective?
No. Absolutely not.
Did I choose it from a soul perspective?
I believe I did.
Dan has helped me to understand this.
He's helped me to understand the soul plans some of us make.

Alongside grief, he has taught me so much
about the unpredictability, the fragility,
as well as the value of this earthly life.

There is so much more to learn,
and I will continue being the eager student he encourages me to be.

His life isn't over.
It didn't end the day he 'died'.
His life, his precious life, his presence, his love,
his lessons, and his teachings continue.
And I am grateful with every fibre of my being....
that I am a part of that continuance.

With deep gratitude
to everyone who is sharing this journey of life and death, of grief and love.

May your onward journey be paved with beautiful blessings.
Much love from the bottom of my heart, to each and every one of you....

Closing words from Spirit....

Please take the hand I'm offering you to guide you through the day
Please allow me to take the lead in my sweet and gentle way

There's nothing that you need to do, no effort on your part
Just watch for the signs I'm sending you, just feel them in your heart

I know you often struggle, I see you trying every day
I smile at the way you listen out, for any words I might have to say

I know our connection is deepening, I know that you notice this too,
Those tingles you're feeling are real, because I'm standing right next to you

Just open up your imagination and picture me standing there
I'm able to reach out and touch you, I love to smooth your hair

I want you to know this is real, despite what you may have thought before
Death simply cannot end a life, we go on forever more.....

Let's learn to invent our own language, something we both understand
Don't worry if you don't believe it at first, just open your heart and take my hand

Those around you, may try to dissuade you, may worry you're not 'letting go'
So we can just keep this between us, those who don't understand, don't need to know

Our bond it just cannot be broken, I don't need to 'move on' in that way, nor do you
Our journey is one of continuance, believe this and know that it's true

In truth we've always been together, through countless lifetimes before
I saw it all in its magnificence, when I opened that heavenly door

I wish I could fully explain it, but I know it's so hard to take in
So just reach out and take my hand, and together, let our new journey begin

The next chapter in 'our book' is now open, the pages, are all blank for now
But in the weeks and months ahead of us, we'll begin to fill them up somehow

If you allow me to, I will show you, that the future will not be all pain
We will learn to communicate & move on together
And I promise you....
Life WILL begin again.

Completing this book has been quite a journey for me, but I have received much encouragement from family and friends along the way, for which I am truly grateful.

And of course, as he always is, my son has been with me, encouraging me from the moment he put the idea of this book into my head.

The photos that I used, to design the front and back cover of this book, were taken near my home

Printed in Great Britain
by Amazon